PAINTED CHAIRS

25 Fresh and Fun Projects

JENNIFER R. FERGUSON
AND JUDITH A. SKINNER

Martingale
& COMPANY
Bothell, Washington

CREDITS

President ❧ Nancy J. Martin
CEO ❧ Daniel J. Martin
Publisher ❧ Jane Hamada
Editorial Director ❧ Mary V. Green
Editorial Project Manager ❧ Tina Cook
Design and Production Manager ❧ Stan Green
Technical Editor ❧ Chris Rich
Copy Editor ❧ Ellen Balstad
Photographer ❧ Brent Kane
Cover and Text Designer ❧ Rohani Design

Painted Chairs: 25 Fresh and Fun Projects
© 2001 by Jennifer R. Ferguson and Judith A. Skinner

Martingale & Company
PO Box 118
Bothell, WA 98041-0118 USA
www.martingale-pub.com

Printed in China
05 04 03 02 01 00   6 5 4 3 2 1

> *Mission Statement*
> We are dedicated to providing quality products
> and service by working together to inspire creativity
> and to enrich the lives we touch.

Library of Congress Cataloging-in-Publication Data

Ferguson, Jennifer R.
   Painted chairs : 25 fresh and fun projects / by Jennifer R. Ferguson and Judith A. Skinner.
      p. cm.
    ISBN 1-56477-340-X
    1. Furniture painting. 2. Furniture finishing. 3. Chairs. 4. Decoration and ornament. I. Skinner, Judith A. II Title.

TT199.4 .F467 2001
683.1—dc21

00-048058

DEDICATION

Without the love and support of our family members, this book would only be a dream. Because they've helped make our dream come true, we—with much love and appreciation—would like to dedicate *Painted Chairs* to our families: Jennifer's husband, Jim, and their children, Ashley and Tyler; and Judy's husband, Don, their children, Donnie, Rex, Corri, and Bob, and their grandchildren, Josh and Samantha.

ACKNOWLEDGMENTS

We'd like to express our immense gratitude to the people who helped create this book:

DecoArt (PO Box 386, Stanford, KY 40484), for supplying their Americana Acrylics paint and other products;

Eagle Brush Company (431 Commerce Park Drive S.E., Suites 100 & 101, Marietta, GA 30060), for supplying all of our artist's brushes;

Friend and employee Patsy Crow, for her endless support and unlimited help;

Friends Mark and Trudy Jensen, for their help with the chair repairs;

Shann Zimmerman Tavares, at Terry's Upholstery (6291 N. Blackstone Avenue, Fresno, CA 93710), for completing our chairs on time and for doing a wonderful job;

And finally, our families, for believing in us and in this book.

Thank you all!

CONTENTS

Introduction   4

Buying a Chair   4

Tools and Supplies   6

Chair Preparation   11

Base-Coat Painting   12

Decorative Painting Techniques   13

Final Touches   19

Projects   20

Planter Chairs   20
Get Wired Up   20
A Bowl of Flowers   23
Hoe, Hoe, Hoe—Off to Work
   We Go   26

Small Wonders   29
Don't Bug Me!   29
Bee Happy   32
Sugar, Spice, and
   Everything Nice   35

Gone Wild   38
Animal Frenzy   38
Home Run   41
Mixed Breed   44

Defined Decor   47
Buzzy Bee   47
Beach Time   50
Farmer's Market   53

Sophisticated Whimsy   56
Harlequin   56
Cherries Jubilee   59
J'Renee's Style   62

Aunt Pittypat's Porch   65
Cobblestone Square   65
Folk-Art Birdhouse   68
Americana with Attitude   71
Aged in Time   74

The Queen Has Arrived   77
All Checked Out   77
Jubee's Throne   80
Spindled Royalty   83

To Fool the Eye   86
A Day in the Garden   86
Take a Note   89
Plant Your Seat   92

Suppliers   95

About the Authors   96

INTRODUCTION

*D*o you own an old chair that's just sitting around—a chair that you'd like to turn into a work of art? Do your dining-room chairs need a fresh look? Have you had difficulty finding chairs that will match or complement the style and color scheme of your home? If so, this book is for you. With its help, you'll soon be creating one-of-a-kind chairs to enhance any room in your house: functional chairs in exactly the right colors for your decor, whimsical chairs that will serve as conversation pieces, and even chairs to enhance your garden. And whether you're a novice painter or an experienced artist, you're about to discover that painting chairs is much easier—and less expensive—than you might think.

In the past, stenciling, faux finishing, and other decorative painting techniques were typically used to add color and interest to interior walls. In recent years, however, more and more people have tried their hands at using these same techniques on chairs. After all, a chair is just another great surface to paint! With a few basic tools and supplies, and the instructions in this book, you can decorate a unique set of dining-room chairs, personalize a chair for a child's room, or make a whimsical planter chair to greet your friends and family at the front door. In fact, once you've learned the basics, there's very little you can't do to, or with, a chair.

Getting started is easy; *Painted Chairs* will guide you through every step of the process. First, you'll learn how to find a suitable chair and how to select your tools and supplies. Then Judy and I will teach you how to prepare both old chairs and new, unfinished chairs for painting. Next, you'll explore the world of decorative painting; Judy and I have explained each technique in detail. Finally, you'll learn how to personalize your decorated chair and protect its painted surfaces. Once you've browsed through these sections of *Painted Chairs,* you'll be ready to choose a project and begin. We hope, of course, that your first chair project inspires you to create many more.

Every one of the projects featured in this book comes with step-by-step instructions that will guide you from start to finish. To help beginning painters achieve professional results, we've named the specific colors that we used to paint each chair, and we've also explained where to place each color and design. Of course, you may want to combine techniques and designs from several different projects to create a uniquely decorated chair of your own.

BUYING A CHAIR

*I*f you'd like to start with a brand-new chair, visit your local unfinished-furniture store. We have several of these stores in our area and have even purchased two unfinished chairs for this book (the "Bee Happy" chair shown on page 33, which was created for the newest member of Judy's family; and the "Harlequin" chair on page 56).

Another option is to buy a used chair. Looking for used chairs can be an art in itself. Most of the chairs in this book were rare finds—used chairs that we gathered during our travels.

Sometimes Judy and I take special chair-hunting trips, but even when we're just on a business trip, we're always on the lookout for another chair. One can never have too many!

Yard sales often yield great chairs at reasonable prices. Stores that sell antiques and collectibles are also good sources for old chairs to paint. You'll need to search through these stores carefully, though, because many of the pieces in them are antiques that are just too valuable to be painted. Over the years, we've also found chairs at thrift shops, junk stores, furniture refinishing shops, and used furniture stores.

Once you've found the chair of your choice, you'll need to decide what you're willing to pay for it. Most dealers will come down a little on the cost, so always ask, "Is this your friendliest price?" Personally, we think haggling over the price is half the fun of finding a chair, and sometimes we simply won't purchase one unless we're given the chance to negotiate a little.

Remember to look in your attic, around your house, and in your garage and backyard, too. You never know where you might find a chair that needs a new look.

AN OVERVIEW OF CHAIR PREPARATION

*A*ll chairs—old or new— require some preparation before you can paint them; we've explained every step of this process on pages 11–12. Meanwhile, take a look at the summary that follows. The step labeled with a "P" is one that Judy and I usually have a professional do for us. By all means, tackle it yourself if you like!

Step Four: Repair the chair as necessary and sand away any visible glue.
Step Five: Fill cracks and dents with wood putty, and sand the putty smooth.
Step Six: Apply one even coat of primer and sand it lightly.
Step Seven: Apply several coats of gesso, sanding each coat very lightly.

OLD CHAIRS

Step One: If the chair seat is upholstered, remove the upholstered portions and set them aside.
Step Two (P): If you want the wood grain to show through your final finish, or if the old paint or varnish is chipping or flaking, you may want to take the chair to a professional for stripping. Sand the chair after it has been stripped.
Step Three: If the old finish is worn but relatively smooth, and if you don't want the wood grain to show through the final finish, sand the chair instead of stripping it. A chair that has been stripped must also be sanded.

NEW, UNFINISHED CHAIRS

Step One: If the chair seat is upholstered, remove the upholstered portions and set them aside.
Step Two: Sand the chair.
Step Three: Apply one coat of wood sealer over the entire chair, and several coats over any knots. Sand the dry sealer lightly.
Step Four: Fill all nail, screw, and staple holes with putty; then sand the chair again.
Step Five: Apply one coat of gesso and sand it lightly.

TOOLS AND SUPPLIES

In this section, we've provided two different lists of the tools and supplies we've used to prepare and paint the chairs in this book. No matter what your chair looks like before you begin or how you plan to paint it, you'll need everything in the first list, titled "Required Tools and Supplies."

The second list, "Technique-Specific Tools and Supplies," describes the products and items used for specific painting techniques. Deciding which ones you'll need is easy. Just take a look at the instructions for your selected project; you'll find what you need listed there.

REQUIRED TOOLS AND SUPPLIES

Most of the items and products in this list are available from craft and art-supply stores or through mail-order suppliers. Others can be found at your local home-improvement store. (See "Suppliers" on page 95.)

Drop Cloth or Newspapers

As you work on your chair, protect your floor or work surface with a drop cloth or several layers of newspaper.

Sandpaper and Sanding Pads

Purchase sandpaper in several different grits or degrees of "roughness," from extra fine to coarse, for sanding bare wood, old finishes, primers, sealers, gesso, and acrylic base coats. Sanding pads are oval or round pads that function just like sandpaper; they also come in different grits.

A handheld electric sander, although not required, will cut through any finish rapidly. Keep in mind that electric sanders can't cope with carved relief surfaces; you'll need to sand these by hand.

Goggles and a Respirator or Dust Mask

Whenever you're sanding, work in a well-ventilated area (preferably outdoors) and wear a respirator or dust mask. Inhaling the airborne particles created during sanding isn't good for your health. Goggles will protect your eyes.

Tack Cloth and Lint-Free Rags

After sanding a chair, you'll use these to wipe away the dust that remains.

Wood Putty

Wood putty serves to fill cracks, chips, and dents, as well as holes above nails, screws, and staples.

Wood Sealer

If your chair is new and unfinished, coat it with water-based wood sealer to help prevent warping and to prevent knots in the wood from bleeding pitch into finishes applied over them.

Primer

You'll brush a water-based primer onto bare wood to help seal it and over old finishes to prevent them from bleeding through. Primers also help subsequent layers of paint bond properly. We have one warning, however, regarding primers. Finishes on old chairs are often oil-based. If you choose to sand down the finish on an old chair rather than have the chair stripped, and if you're not sure whether the old finish is oil- or water-based, use an oil-based primer. (A water-based primer may not adhere properly.)

Gesso

Gesso is a very thick, water-based artist's primer that yields an opaque, smooth finish. You'll brush it onto your chair before you apply the base coats.

Artist's Brushes

Gather an assortment of flat, round, and angle-tipped artist's brushes, from $\frac{1}{4}$" to 1" wide. These brushes will yield smoother finishes than ordinary paintbrushes.

Acrylic Artist's Paints

You'll use these paints, which are available in two-ounce bottles, for all your decorative painting. For most chairs, one two-ounce bottle of each color will do. (The "Acrylic Paints" list that comes with each set of project instructions will let you know if you need more.) All the acrylic paints we've used on the chairs in this book are DecoArt Americana Acrylics. Please note that acrylic colors are darker when they're dry than they are in their bottles. To test a color, brush some of the paint onto a piece of paper and let it dry.

Extender

Extenders, which come in two-ounce bottles, extend the drying time of acrylic paints. Adding a drop or two to each color you use when you're stenciling will make the paint more manageable and will help create smooth finished surfaces. You'll only need one bottle, even if you make every project in this book.

Precut Stencils

A precut stencil is a sheet of plastic with a pattern of holes (or windows) in it. You'll add design motifs and lettering to your chair by applying paint through the windows. Stencils usually come in plastic bags. Save the bags if you can; they'll help protect your stencils when you're not using them.

Removable Tape and a Burnisher

To help affix stencils to your chair and to mask off areas that you don't want to paint, removable painter's tape works well. To burnish (or press down) the edges of the tape, use a burnishing tool or the edge of a plastic card, such as a credit card.

Stencil Brushes

You'll need several stencil brushes, ranging from ¼" to 1" in width. Unlike artist's brushes, stencil brushes have stiff bristles and blunt ends.

Paint Palette

You'll never dip a brush directly into a bottle of paint. Instead, you'll pick up the paint from a palette. Saucers, paper plates, and ice cube trays make adequate substitutes.

Paper Towels

Use folded paper towels to remove excess paint from stencil brushes, and, when you're creating sponged faux finishes, from your sea wool sponge.

Paint Pen

For signing your finished masterpiece, a fine-tipped black paint pen is convenient and easy to handle.

Varnish

To protect your finished chair, you'll apply several coats of water-based varnish to it. Use an interior varnish for chairs that will rest indoors and an exterior varnish for chairs that you plan to set outdoors. You'll also need varnish to create antique finishes.

Scrubber Sponge and AC's Acrylic Craft Paint Remover

A kitchen sponge with one rough surface will help remove paint from stencils. AC's Acrylic Craft Paint Remover, a solution designed to remove acrylic paints, is available from mail-order suppliers. (See "Suppliers" on page 95.)

Brush Cleaner/Conditioner and a Brush Scrubber

To clean your stencil brushes, use a brush cleaner/conditioner and a brush scrubber. The cleaner/conditioner also works with artist's brushes. Brush scrubbers are small plastic implements with thin teeth that help remove paint from stencil-brush bristles; you can order one through a mail-order supplier. (See "Suppliers" on page 95.)

Water Basin and Small Plastic Bags

Make sure you have a water basin on hand, as well as several small plastic bags to keep your brush bristles from drying out as you work.

TECHNIQUE-SPECIFIC TOOLS AND SUPPLIES

To find out which of these items you'll need, just refer to the "Tools and Supplies" list that accompanies your selected project. The project list will also include odds and ends such as decorative accessories.

Screwdrivers and Wood Glue

To remove the seat from a chair, you'll need a Phillips-head or flat-bladed screwdriver. To reattach the seat, use the original screws and some wood glue.

Fabric

For upholstered chairs, you'll need new fabric. To remove any sizing and chemicals that might prevent the paint from adhering properly, always wash the fabric before you begin. Make sure you purchase enough fabric to cover the upholstered seat or back; each piece should be several inches longer and wider than the exposed seat or back surface.

Fabric Painting Medium

This medium, which comes in two ounce bottles, helps acrylic paints adhere to fabrics and also helps the paint from becoming stiff after it has dried.

Transparent Fabric Medium

To create a translucent wash for fabrics, you'll mix transparent fabric medium with acrylic paint.

Repositionable Spray Adhesive and Cardboard

To help hold a piece of fabric flat as you stencil it, use spray adhesive to affix the fabric to a sheet of smooth cardboard.

Press Cloth and an Iron

After stenciling fabric and allowing the paint to dry, heat-set the paint by placing a press cloth (a piece of cotton or organza) over the fabric and heating the cloth with an iron.

Gel Stains

You'll brush these translucent stains over painted and varnished surfaces and then wipe them to give your decorated chair an antique, distressed appearance. Gel stains are available in two-ounce bottles. Judy and I use DecoArt Americana Gel Stain (DS30).

Faux Glazing Medium

You'll add this medium to acrylic paints to create sponged, stippled, and marbleized finishes. The pigment-free medium, available in eight-ounce (and larger) bottles, adds translucency to the painted finish.

Natural Sea Wool Sponges

For sponged faux finishes, you'll need one or more natural sea wool sponges. These sponges are available from craft stores, and they are much softer than ordinary sea sponges.

Latex or Rubber Gloves

When you're using a sponge to apply paint, protect your hands with latex or rubber gloves.

Special Brushes

For some projects, you'll need a #1 liner brush (a fine-tipped artist's brush). For a couple of projects, you'll also need an artist's fan (a brush with bristles that spread into a fan shape); and a wing, comb, or rake brush. (Different manufacturers call these brushes by different names, but wing, comb, and rake brushes are all similar.) A 1"-wide, wedge-shaped foam brush will come in handy for painting stripes.

Cotton Swabs and an Embossing Tool

For creating large La De Da Dots (see page 18), cotton swabs work well. For smaller dots, use one end of an embossing tool. (This crafter's tool, which is usually used to emboss paper, is simply a stick with a small, hard metal ball at one or both ends.) The tip of a brush handle will also work as a dot applicator.

Watercolor Pencils

Watercolor pencils are ideal for marking stripes and for sketching lettering. Use light-colored pencils so the watercolor lines won't show through the paint that covers them.

Transparent Graph Ruler

You'll use a 2"-wide, 18"-long graph ruler and a watercolor pencil to mark off areas for painted stripes. Because you can see through them, these rulers are especially useful when you're trying to align one marked line with another.

Crackle Medium

To create a crackle effect, you'll need some of this clear liquid, which is available in eight-ounce bottles. You'll apply the medium on top of an opaque base coat, allow it to dry, and then brush another coat of paint over it.

Empty Two-Ounce Bottle with Lid

For some projects, you'll need an empty paint bottle in which to mix two different colors of paint.

CHAIR PREPARATION

*B*efore you paint a chair, whether it's a new, unfinished chair or an old chair that's already been painted, you'll need to prepare the surface, or the paint you apply won't adhere properly.

PREPARING AN OLD CHAIR

Before you begin, protect your floor or work surface with a drop cloth or several layers of newspaper, and gather your tools and supplies.

If your chair has an upholstered seat, you'll probably be able to remove it yourself; most seats are simply attached with screws. Set the seat aside. When you've painted your chair and new fabric, you'll take the old seat, the chair, and the fabric to an upholsterer. (See "Final Touches" on page 19.) If the chair back is also upholstered, have the upholsterer remove it for you.

Most chairs don't need stripping, but stripping is warranted if your chair is covered with many layers of paint or finish that are chipped or flaking. You'll also need to strip your chair if you want the wood grain to show through the paint you apply. We usually have a professional strip our chairs, but if you'd like to do it yourself, you'll find the required tools and supplies at a home-improvement or paint store.

Sanding will usually work to remove all loose particles of the existing finish and to roughen the surface of any finish that remains. New paint won't adhere to a slick finished surface. Start with rough-grit paper or pads, and use finer grits as the work progresses. If possible, do your sanding outdoors; you'll generate a lot of dust as you work. And remember to wear your goggles and a respirator or dust mask.

When you're finished, wipe the chair with rags or a tack cloth to remove any dust. (Note that even stripped chairs must be sanded.)

If your chair is rickety, have a woodworker repair it for you. Sand the chair to remove all visible glue, and wipe away any sanding dust with a tack cloth or rags. Then use wood putty to fill any holes, pits, or dents in the chair's surface. Allow the putty to dry and sand its surface lightly to make it level with the surrounding wood.

The next step is priming. Using a water-based primer and a flat artist's brush—$1/2$" or 1" wide—apply a thin first coat of primer to the entire chair. (If your chair still has the remnants of an old finish on it, and if you think that finish might be oil-based, use an oil-based primer for this step.) For the smoothest possible finish, keep your brush strokes going in the same direction. After the primer has dried, sand it lightly with your finest-grit sandpaper. Then wipe the chair with a tack cloth.

Now you must apply several coats of gesso on top of the primer—as many coats as necessary to achieve coverage that is smooth and opaque. Use an artist's brush to apply each coat, and keep your strokes going in the same direction. Allow each coat to dry; then sand it lightly with your finest-grit sandpaper. Wipe the chair off before applying the next coat.

PREPARING A NEW, UNFINISHED CHAIR

Remove any upholstered parts and set them aside. (An upholsterer can help if you have trouble.) Sand the chair well with fine-grit sandpaper, preferably outdoors, and remember to wear goggles and a dust mask or respirator. Move the sandpaper in the same direction as the wood grain rather than sanding against—or perpendicular to—the grain. (The grain appears as streaks in the wood.) Remove all rough edges and traces of glue, and smooth all surfaces. Wipe the chair with a tack cloth or rags when you're finished.

Next, using a ½"- or 1"-wide artist's brush, apply a thin, even coat of wood sealer to the entire chair. The sealer will help prevent warping and will also raise the wood grain slightly, which in turn will help your gesso and paint adhere well. Allow the sealer to dry, sand it very lightly with fine-grit sandpaper, and wipe the chair again with a tack cloth. (Apply several coats of sealer over any knots in the wood, drying and sanding lightly between each application so the knots won't bleed pitch through the gesso and paint.)

Now fill any holes, cracks, or gaps with wood putty. Allow the putty to dry, sand it lightly with fine-grit sandpaper, and wipe the chair off with a tack cloth.

To prime the sealed chair, apply one coat of gesso, brushing with the wood grain rather than against it. Allow the gesso to dry and sand it very lightly with fine-grit sandpaper to smooth its surface. Wipe the chair off with a tack cloth.

BASE-COAT PAINTING

Your chair is now ready for the first stage of decorative painting, which consists of applying opaque acrylic paints. Each set of project instructions specifies which base-coat colors to use and where to apply them.

Pour a little paint onto your palette and work some of it into a flat artist's brush. Brush the paint onto the chair, keeping your brush strokes moving in the direction of the wood grain. If the paint won't brush on smoothly, dip your brush into water to moisten it slightly before working the paint into the bristles.

Allow the first coat of paint to dry. If its surface isn't smooth, use your finest-grit sandpaper to smooth it, removing as little paint as possible. Apply as many coats as necessary to achieve opaque coverage, letting each one dry before applying the next.

Applying many different base-coat colors side by side requires some care—and a steady hand! Using a small artist's brush with an angled tip will help you apply the colors neatly and evenly right next to each other. Let each color dry before you apply the next. If you accidentally brush one color on top of another or brush an unwanted color onto an adjacent, unpainted area, first pick up as much of the excess paint as possible with a dry artist's brush. Then scrub off some more with a dampened cotton swab, and repaint this area as necessary.

DECORATIVE PAINTING TECHNIQUES

*I*n this section, you'll find complete instructions for all the decorative painting techniques we've used to decorate our chairs. You certainly don't need to memorize every detail; just turn back to these pages whenever you need to refresh your memory.

STENCILING

Stenciling is a remarkably easy painting technique. Each set of project instructions specifies which stencils to use, where to place them on the chair, and which colors to apply. For all the projects in this book, we've used Stencilled Garden stencils; these are available at many craft stores and from mail-order suppliers. (See "Suppliers" on page 95.)

Positioning the Stencil

Position your stencil, locating its open design portions exactly where you'd like the painted design to appear. Then tape the outer edges of the stencil to the chair with removable painter's tape.

Positioning the stencil

Loading the Stencil Brush

Pour a little paint onto your palette, add one to two drops of extender, and use the handle end of your stencil brush to mix the extender in well. Next, holding your stencil brush straight up, pick up a small amount of paint with the tips of the brush bristles. Then work the paint into the bristles by wiping them in a circular motion on a clean section of the palette.

One trick to successful stenciling is having only the tiniest amount of paint on your brush bristles. To remove the excess paint, hold the brush upright and with a firm, circular motion, rub the bristles onto a folded paper towel. Then, on a clean portion of the paper towel, wipe the brush in an **X** motion to remove excess paint from the outer bristles.

Mixing paint and extender

Working paint into brush bristles

Removing paint from brush

Applying the Paint

For a smooth stenciled surface, "swirling" is the best technique to use. Hold your stencil brush perpendicular to the chair's surface and apply the paint by moving the bristle ends in tiny circles. To add texture and depth to a stenciled design, hold the brush perpendicular to the chair's surface, but instead of swirling the bristles, apply the paint by dabbing the brush straight up and down—a process known as "stippling" or "pouncing." Whether you're swirling or stippling, always use a light touch.

To create shading within each stenciled design area, first create sharp, crisp edges by applying paint lightly all the way around the outer edges of the design window. As you work, blend paint into the inner design area but apply less pressure to the brush—and less paint. By varying the pressure you apply to your brush and the amount of time you spend stenciling a given area, you can achieve a wide range of values with a single color.

Stenciling with one color

For added contrast within a design, use more than one color. Let each color dry before applying the next, use a different brush for each color, and leave the stencil in place until you've applied all the colors. (Once you've removed a stencil, it's very difficult to replace it in exactly the same position.) To keep the paint-dampened bristles of your brushes from drying out as you work on a project, place each brush in a small plastic bag until you need to use it again.

Shading with two colors

Here's one important tip: When you're stenciling on top of a dark base-coat color, stencil the entire design in white paint first. Then apply your colors over the white. If you skip this step, your stenciled colors won't show up on the dark background.

Stenciling on Fabric

To hold fabric flat as you stencil it, apply repositionable spray adhesive to a piece of smooth cardboard. (The cardboard doesn't have to be as large as your fabric; you'll only stencil one section of the fabric at a time.) Gently press the fabric onto the adhesive-coated cardboard, and tape your stencil in place.

Mix one part fabric painting medium with two parts paint on your palette. Using stencil brushes, apply this paint mixture to the cardboard-backed section of the fabric and allow the paint to dry. Then peel the fabric up and reposition it so the next portion you want to stencil is held flat against the cardboard. Repeat this process until you've finished all stenciling. After the paint has dried completely, heat-set the paint by placing a press cloth on top of the fabric and pressing the cloth with a warm iron.

Stenciling on fabric

Cleaning and Storing Stencils and Brushes

After using a stencil, clean it as soon as possible. The longer the paint stays on the stencil, the harder it will be to remove. One cleaning method is to use hot water and a bit of elbow grease. Place the stencil under running hot water and rub it gently with a rag, a paper towel, or the rough side of a sponge. Another way to clean a stencil is with AC's Acrylic Craft Paint Remover. (See "Suppliers" on page 95.) Place the stencil in the sink, pour the cleaner over it, let the cleaner sit for a minute or two, and then gently scrub off the paint with a scrubber. Rinse the stencil with hot water to remove the cleaner. Unfortunately, the process of cleaning stencils is hard on them and makes it all too easy to damage them, too. Judy and I recommend using the acrylic paint remover rather than water because you won't have to rub as hard to remove the paint.

To dry a stencil after cleaning it, place it on a towel and either let it air dry or pat it dry with a paper towel. Store clean stencils in their original plastic bags, stacking the bags to keep the stencils flat.

To clean a stencil brush, moisten it with water, pour a little brush cleaner/conditioner over the bristles, and scrub the brush gently over the surface of a brush scrubber.

COLOR WASHING

A color wash is simply diluted paint; it's usually applied on top of an opaque base coat to create a faded, uneven look. (The "Get Wired Up" chair on page 20 is one exception; the color wash on this chair is applied directly to the gesso coat.) To make the wash, first pour a small amount of paint onto your palette. Then, using an artist's brush to transfer water from the basin to the palette, gradually mix a solution of colored water.

Brush the wash onto the chair with an artist's brush. Use long, sweeping strokes that follow the wood grain and that extend from one edge of the area you want to wash to the other. If you're new to this technique, practice on a sheet of posterboard with the same wash colors you plan to use on your chair. First apply an opaque base coat to the posterboard and let it dry. Then mix and apply the wash. To darken the wash, just add more paint to the mixture on your palette; to lighten the wash, add more water.

Color-washed surface

ANTIQUE FINISHES

To create a "distressed" or antique look, first apply one coat of varnish over the opaque base coats on all parts of the chair that you'd like to antique. Allow the varnish to dry. Then, working on one small area at a time, use an artist's brush to apply a gel stain over the varnish, brushing in the same direction as you did when applying the base coats. While the gel is still wet, use a rag to wipe it. As you wipe, the base-coat colors will darken and acquire an aged, distressed look. For a darker finish, apply several coats of the gel stain, wiping after each coat and allowing the stain to dry before applying the next coat.

Applying a coat of varnish before you add the gel stain gives you more working time and control as you apply and wipe off the gel. A gel applied directly to the base coat will "grab" the paint and will stain it darker than you might want; the varnish slows down this grabbing process, leaving you more time to create the look you want to achieve.

If you like, you can mask adjacent areas with removable tape before you apply varnish and gel stain. The tape will help protect these areas from accidental smears, but it won't

prevent the varnish and gel from creeping under the tape's edges.

Antique-finished surface

SPONGED FAUX FINISHES

Sponged faux finishes are applied on top of base coats to create variegated textures and colors. To begin, mix paint and faux glazing medium on a palette; in most cases, you'll add no more than 5 to 25 percent paint to the medium. Use the handle of an artist's brush to mix them together. Next, dampen a natural sea wool sponge with water, wring out all excess moisture, and dip the sponge into the glaze mixture. To work the mixture into the sponge, use a circular motion to rub the sponge on a clean section of your palette. Then dab the sponge onto a paper towel to off-load some of the glaze mixture.

Using a light touch and a stippling motion, sponge the mixture onto the chair. Allow the sponged glaze to dry thoroughly. If you like, you may apply more coats, letting each one dry before applying the next.

Sponged surface

MARBLEIZED FINISHES

For a marbleized effect, first use a sea wool sponge to apply several coats of glaze-and-paint mixture on top of the base coat. (See the preceding section, "Sponged Faux Finishes.") To create depth and dimension as you do this, use a different color for each coat and allow each one to dry before applying the next. When the last coat is dry, pour a little paint-and-glaze mixture onto your palette, dip a #1 liner brush into it, and drag the brush across the sponged glaze in a jagged motion to create the marble veins.

Marbleized surface

CRACKLE FINISHES

A crackle finish is one in which thin lines of a base-coat color appear through cracks in a topcoat of another color. To create this effect, first apply the layers of base coat to your chair, keeping in mind that the color you use here will be the one that appears through the cracks in the topcoat. When the final base coat is dry, pour some crackle medium onto your palette. Using an artist's brush, apply the medium over the area that you want to crackle. The thinner the coat of medium, the smaller the cracks will be and the more subtle the finished effect. For larger, more pronounced cracks, apply a thicker coat. Allow the medium to dry.

Next, brush a coat of paint over the crackle medium. The stronger the contrast between the color you choose for this topcoat and the color of your base coat, the more noticeable the finished crackle effect will be. Be very careful to apply the topcoat with long, even brush strokes and never to brush back over any topcoat paint that you've already applied. The moment you start applying the topcoat, it will begin to react with the crackle medium. If you brush back over any topcoat paint that has started to dry, your brush will lift the topcoat right off the chair. Short of sanding your chair and starting over, there's no way to repair a botched crackle job, so take care to apply the topcoat by running your brush strokes in a single direction, one stroke next to another.

Crackle-finished surface

STRIPES

To make stripes, start by measuring and marking off the stripes with a transparent graph ruler and a light-colored watercolor pencil. Although you can paint the marked stripes freehand, you may want to mask their edges instead. To do so, cut pieces of removable tape and position them just along the outer edges of each marked stripe. Using a burnisher, press down the edges of the tape to help prevent paint from seeping under them.

On your palette, mix four parts paint with one part water. (This diluted mixture will yield soft-colored stripes.) Then, with a foam brush, apply the paint to the area between the two pieces of tape. Remove the tape after the paint has dried. If watercolor pencil marks are visible, carefully wipe them away with a damp rag.

Step 1: Mark your stripe.

Step 2: Align removable tape with the marked lines; then burnish the tape.

Step 3: Paint your stripe.

Step 4: Remove the tape after the paint has dried

LA DE DA DOTS

La De Da Dots are simply raised dots of paint. Pour a little paint onto your palette. To make large dots, dip a cotton swab into the paint and dab it onto the chair to release a raised drop of paint. To ensure that the dots are raised rather than flat, pick up more paint from your palette for each dot you make. For small dots, use one end of an embossing tool as an applicator. The tip of a brush handle will also work.

Sometimes, beginners have trouble placing dots, bunching them up in some areas and scattering them too far apart in others. Here's a tip that will help: Begin by imagining a small diamond or triangle, right in the middle of the area that you want to cover with dots. Apply a dot to each of the diamond or triangle's corners. Now visualize another diamond or triangle next to the first one. Apply dots to the corners of this second diamond or triangle. By continuing to apply dots to the corners of imaginary diamond or triangle shapes, you'll find that you end up scattering your dots surprisingly evenly.

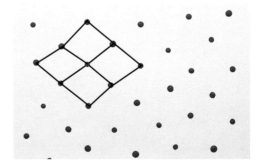

Small La De Da Dots made with diamond shapes

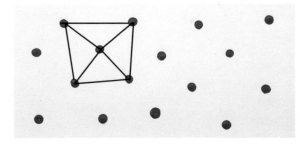

Large La De Da Dots made with triangle shapes

FINAL TOUCHES

We've always found that it's fun to personalize our chairs by signing and dating the underside of each seat. When Judy's grandson, Josh, was very young, he would try to say "Judy" and out would come "Jubee" instead, so Judy signs all her work both with the word "Ju" and with a stenciled bee—to symbolize the word "Jubee." I sign each chair with something different. If the chair will be a gift to someone, I often write a personal message. At other times, I just sign off with "J. Ferguson" and a date.

We also save any item that provides information about a chair's history, whether it's an inscribed plate fastened to an old chair or documents that indicate who made the chair and where it was built.

The next step to completing your project—applying varnish—is very important, as the varnish will protect all the work you've put into your masterpiece. Use a water-based varnish and apply it with a flat artist's brush. To avoid drips and runs, apply at least three thin, even coats, allowing each coat to dry thoroughly before applying the next.

If your painted chair had an upholstered seat or back, visit your upholsterer after the varnish is dry. Bring the chair, your new fabric, and the old upholstered seat or back with you. The upholsterer can make a new seat or back if necessary and will use your fabric to cover it before attaching it to the chair.

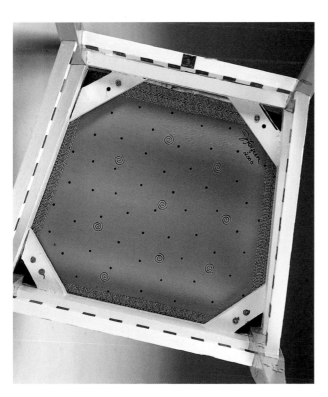

Sign each chair.

ANATOMY OF A CHAIR

Parts of a Chair You May Not Know

Back slats are the chair parts that support your back when you're sitting.

Skirt rails are the boards that rest just beneath the seat to form a "skirt" around its bottom edges.

Stretchers are the narrow pieces that run from one leg to another. They keep the legs from spreading apart or collapsing inward.

We discovered this chair during one of the first "junking" trips that we took just to find chairs. Because its seat was missing, it was the perfect choice for a planter. A unique conversation piece, this whimsical project never fails to get more than its share of amazed looks and amused comments from our friends and customers. What better way could you find to greet people at your own front door?

GET WIRED UP

TOOLS AND SUPPLIES

Required tools and supplies (see pages 6–8)
Screwdriver
Cotton swabs
Chicken wire (small mesh)
Staple gun and staples
Coconut plant liner
Plastic liner or planting soil
Green moss
Plants of your choice, in their containers
Raffia
Miniature watering can
Acrylic paints

To reproduce the photographed chair, use the DecoArt Americana paints listed below, or substitute other acrylic paints for a different look.

✓French Vanilla (DA184)
✓White (DA01)
  Napa Red (DA165)
✓French Mauve (DA186)
  Raspberry (DA28)
  Summer Lilac (DA189)
  Black (DA67)
  Pansy Lavender (DA154)
  Evergreen (DA82)
  Mauve (DA26)
  Moon Yellow (DA07)
  Hauser Medium Green (DA132)
  Easy Blend Charcoal Grey (DEB28)

Stencils

If you'd like to reproduce this chair exactly as it's shown, use the Stencilled Garden stencils listed here; they're available at specialty stencil stores and through mail-order suppliers. (See "Suppliers" on page 95.) For a different look, just substitute other stencils.

Girly's Flowers (TSG175)
Girly's Flower Border (TSG122)
Ashley's Tea Party (TSG183)
Lil Checks (TSG707)
Summertime (TSG176)
Bee Happy (TSG177)
Cherries Jubilee (TSG184)
Checkerboards (TSG706)

INSTRUCTIONS

1. Remove and discard the chair seat, and prepare your chair for painting. (See "Chair Preparation" on pages 11–12.)
2. Apply as many base coats as necessary to achieve smooth, opaque coverage on all chair parts except the center back slat. (See "Base-Coat Painting" on page 12.) For correct color placement, refer to the photos and to the "Base-Coat Color Guide" provided on the next page.
3. On the center back slat, apply a French Mauve color wash directly to the gesso primer. (See "Color Washing" on pages 15–16.)
4. Stencil the designs. Refer to the photos as necessary and to the "Stencil Color Guide" provided on the next page. For detailed stenciling instructions, see "Stenciling" on pages 13–15.

Back slats

5. With a cotton swab, apply Black La De Da Dots to the inner edges of the back legs and the upper edge of the back skirt rail. (See "La De Da Dots" on page 18.) Apply White La De Da Dots to the front legs and center back slat, as shown in the photos.

BASE-COAT COLOR GUIDE

CHAIR PARTS	COLORS
Top back slat	French Vanilla
Back legs, skirt rails	White
Stretchers (left, center, and right)	Napa Red, French Mauve, Raspberry
Front legs (top to bottom)	Raspberry, Summer Lilac, French Vanilla, Black, French Mauve, Pansy Lavender, French Vanilla, Raspberry

6. Sign your chair and allow all the paint to dry for several days. Then protect your work by applying at least 3 coats of varnish. (See "Final Touches" on page 19.) If your chair will be placed outdoors, remember to use an exterior varnish.

7. Cut a piece of chicken wire that is large enough to fit into the seat area and to form a basket beneath it. Using your staple gun, attach the chicken wire to the inner edges of the skirt rails.

8. Spread the coconut plant liner in the chicken-wire basket. If you plan to set the chair indoors, cover the coconut plant liner with a layer of plastic liner to help prevent water from dripping out of the basket. Place your plant containers in the lined basket and fill all open areas with green moss. When your plants are thirsty, just remove the containers and replace them after watering. If you'd like to place your chair outdoors, line the wire basket with coconut plant liner; then add a layer of planting soil. Remove your plants from their containers, plant them in the soil, and cover the soil with a layer of green moss.

9. Accessorize by using raffia to attach a miniature watering can to the chair's top back slat.

STENCIL COLOR GUIDE

CHAIR PARTS	STENCILS	COLORS
Top back slat	Girly's Flowers, placed randomly	French Mauve, Evergreen, Mauve
Center back slat	Girly's Flower Border	French Vanilla, Moon Yellow, Evergreen, White
Back legs	Ashley's Tea Party	Napa Red, White, Moon Yellow, Evergreen
	Lil Checks	Black
Outer faces of side skirt rails	Summertime	Napa Red, Hauser Medium Green, Black
	Bees from Bee Happy	Moon Yellow, Black, Easy Blend Charcoal Grey
Outer faces of front and back skirt rails	Cherries Jubilee	Napa Red, Evergreen
Upper edges of side and front skirt rails	Checkerboards: ¾"	Black

A BOWL OF FLOWERS

TOOLS AND SUPPLIES

Required tools and supplies (see pages 6–8)
Screwdriver
Faux glazing medium
Natural sea wool sponge
Embossing tool
Preplanted flower bowl
Acrylic paints

To reproduce the photographed chair, use the DecoArt Americana paints listed below, or substitute other acrylic paints for a different look.

Black (DA67)
Camel (DA191)
Light Buttermilk (DA164)
Honey Brown (DA163)
Wisteria (DA211)
Violet Haze (DA197)
Evergreen (DA82)
White (DA01)

Stencils

If you'd like to reproduce this chair exactly as it's shown, use the Stencilled Garden stencils listed here; they're available at specialty stencil stores and through mail-order suppliers. (See "Suppliers" on page 95.) For a different look, just substitute other stencils.

Wild Animal Print (TSG128)
Classic Rope (TSG154)
Girly's Flowers (TSG175)
Penny's Poultry Gone Wild (TSG142)

INSTRUCTIONS

1. Remove the seat from your chair. Have a woodworker cut a hole in its center to hold your flower bowl; ask him or her to reattach the seat with wood glue and screws.
2. Prepare the chair for painting. (See "Chair Preparation" on pages 11–12.)
3. Apply as many base coats as necessary to achieve smooth, opaque coverage on the entire chair. (See "Base-Coat Painting" on page 12.) For correct color placement, refer to the photos and to the "Base-Coat Color Guide" provided below.
4. Using removable painter's tape, mask off all chair parts that are adjacent to the areas painted with Camel.
5. On your palette, mix 1 part Honey Brown with 3 parts faux glazing medium. Then, using your sea wool sponge, lightly sponge all the Camel-painted areas with the glaze mixture. (See "Sponged Faux Finishes" on page 16.)
6. Stencil the designs. Refer to the photos as necessary and to the "Stencil Color Guide" provided on page 25. For detailed stenciling instructions, see "Stenciling" on pages 13–15.

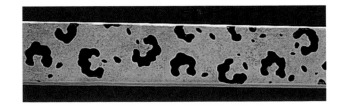

Wild Animal Print stencil used on faux-finished areas

BASE-COAT COLOR GUIDE

CHAIR PARTS	COLORS
Back legs, front stretcher	Black
Top and bottom back slats, front legs, back stretcher, seat	Camel
Center back slats, skirt rails, side stretchers	Light Buttermilk

A customer of mine who is well acquainted with my chair fetish couldn't bring herself to throw this chair away, so she brought it to me for recycling. I knew that it was too old and battered to use as a chair, so I decided to transform it into an easy-maintenance planter chair for my house. I designed it to hold a standard flower bowl that I could remove and replace whenever I liked.

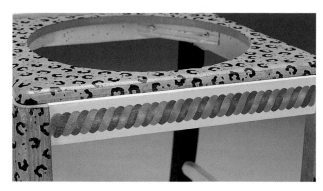

Skirt rail

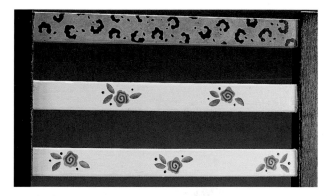

Back slats

Outer edge of back leg

Side view

7. Use an embossing tool to apply Black La De Da Dots around the Girly's Flowers designs on the center back slats. (See "La De Da Dots" on page 18.) For correct placement, refer to the photos.
8. Sign your chair and allow the paint to dry for several days. Then protect your work by applying at least 3 coats of varnish. (See "Final Touches" on page 19.)
9. Insert the flower bowl into the hole in the seat.

STENCIL COLOR GUIDE

CHAIR PARTS	STENCILS	COLORS
All faux-finished areas	Wild Animal Print	Black
Skirt rails	Classic Rope	Wisteria, Violet Haze
Center back slats	Girly's Flowers	Wisteria, Violet Haze, Evergreen
Outer edge of each back leg	Zebra pattern from Penny's Poultry Gone Wild	White

HOE, HOE, HOE— OFF TO WORK WE GO

TOOLS AND SUPPLIES

Required tools and supplies (see pages 6–8)
Screwdriver
Wood glue
Watercolor pencil—any light color
Black paint pen
Embossing tool
Bucket
Rake
Hoe
Epoxy glue
Hammer and awl
Potting soil
Plants
Acrylic paints
> To reproduce the photographed chair, use the DecoArt Americana paints listed below, or substitute other acrylic paints for a different look.

French Vanilla (DA184)
Burnt Orange (DA16)
French Mauve (DA186)
Violet Haze (DA197)
Light Avocado (DA106)
Stencil
> If you'd like to reproduce this chair exactly as it's shown, use the Stencilled Garden stencil listed here; it's available at specialty stencil stores and through mail-order suppliers. (See "Suppliers" on page 95.) For a different look, just substitute a different stencil.

Checkerboards (TSG706)

INSTRUCTIONS

1. Remove the seat from your chair. Have a woodworker make a new seat with a hole in its center or cut a hole in the existing seat. (Make sure the hole will hold your bucket.) Ask the woodworker to attach the new seat to the chair with wood glue and screws.

2. Prepare the seat and chair for painting. (See "Chair Preparation" on pages 11–12.)

3. Apply as many base coats as necessary to achieve smooth, opaque coverage on the entire chair. (See "Base-Coat Painting" on page 12.) For correct color placement, refer to the photos and to the "Base-Coat Color Guide" provided on page 28.

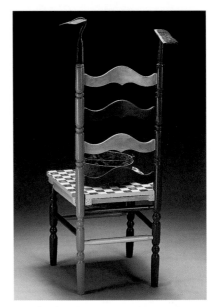

Back view

Checkerboard design on seat

We're Blooming in the Garden

This chair was originally an unsightly gift, but Judy, with her creative eyes and mind, quickly saw its potential. After gathering a rake, hoe, and bucket, she designed a wonderful planter chair and sometimes hangs her small garden tools from its back slats. Judy removed the old woven seat and had a new one made to hold the planter bucket.

BASE-COAT COLOR GUIDE

CHAIR PARTS	COLORS
2 back slats, seat, centers of skirt rails, upper side stretchers, bottom back stretcher	French Vanilla
2 back slats, side stretchers	Burnt Orange
1 back leg, bottom front stretcher	French Mauve
1 back leg, upper front stretcher	Violet Haze
Front legs, upper back stretcher	Light Avocado

Back slats

Corner of skirt rail

4. Prepare a Burnt Orange color wash. Apply it to two of the back slats and to the centers of the skirt rails. (See "Color Washing" on pages 15–16.)

5. Using Burnt Orange, stencil the 1½" checkerboard design on top of the seat. (See "Stenciling" on pages 13–15.)

6. With a watercolor pencil, sketch the sentence on the chair's back slats. When you're happy with your lettering, trace over the letters with a paint pen.

7. Using an embossing tool, apply French Mauve La De Da Dots to the skirt-rail corners. (See "La De Da Dots" on page 18.)

8. Sign your chair and allow the paint to dry for several days. Then protect your work by applying at least 3 coats of varnish. (See "Final Touches" on page 19.) If your chair will be set outdoors, be sure to use exterior varnish.

9. Remove the handles from the rake and hoe; then use epoxy glue to attach the metal heads to the back legs.

10. To provide drainage, punch holes in the bottom of the bucket with a hammer and awl.

11. Place the bucket into the hole in the seat, fill the bucket with potting soil, and set your plants in the soil.

DON'T BUG ME!

TOOLS AND SUPPLIES

Required tools and supplies (see pages 6–8)
Empty 2-ounce bottle with lid
Faux glazing medium
Natural sea wool sponge
#1 liner brush
Long-handled bug net (optional)
Raffia (optional)
Acrylic paints

To reproduce the photographed chair, use the DecoArt Americana paints listed below, or substitute other acrylic paints for a different look.

White (DA01)—2 bottles
Country Blue (DA41)
Olive Green (DA56)
Evergreen (DA82)
Khaki Tan (DA173)
Easy Blend Charcoal Grey (DEB28)
Metallic Green Pearl (DA122)
Metallic Ice Blue (DA75)
Black (DA67)
Tomato Red (DA169)
Moon Yellow (DA07)
Marigold (DA194)
Hauser Light Green (DA131)
Hauser Medium Green (DA132)
Violet Haze (DA197)
Soft Black (DA155)
Charcoal Grey (DA88)
Santa Red (DA170)

Stencils

If you'd like to reproduce this chair exactly as it's shown, use the Stencilled Garden stencils listed here; they're available at specialty stencil stores and through mail-order suppliers. (See "Suppliers" on page 95.) For a different look, just substitute other stencils.

Complete Alphabet (TSG810)
Whimsy Critters (TSG828)
Garden Critters (TSG140)
Butterflies (TSG701)
Creepy Crawlers (TSG699)

INSTRUCTIONS

1. Prepare your chair for painting. (See "Chair Preparation" on pages 11–12.)

2. The base-coat color on this chair is a mixture of Country Blue and White. Start by filling four-fifths of your empty bottle with White paint. Then add Country Blue to create a very pale blue, shaking the mixture well. (Acrylic colors are darker when they're dry than they are in their bottles. To test a color, brush some of the paint onto a piece of paper and let it dry.)

3. Apply as many coats of the pale blue paint as necessary to achieve smooth, opaque coverage on the entire chair. (See "Base-Coat Painting" on page 12.)

4. On your palette, mix 1 part White paint with 1 part faux glazing medium. Then, with your natural sea wool sponge, lightly sponge the entire chair. (See "Sponged Faux Finishes" on page 16.)

5. The grass blades on the chair legs are Olive Green and Evergreen. Start by pouring a small (nickel-sized) pool of Olive Green onto your palette. Add a couple of drops of extender to the paint, and enough water to make it the texture of light cream. Diluting the paint in this manner will help you achieve smooth, continuous brush strokes.

6. To paint each Olive Green blade of grass, hold your #1 liner brush perpendicular to the chair's surface. Start at the bottom of the leg and brush upward, lifting the brush up at the end of the stroke.

$\mathcal{J}$ found this chair, covered with dirt and insects, in Clark and Peggy's (my in-laws') woodpile and saved it from death by fire. I thought a stenciled bug motif would look cute on it and decided to make it a child's chair. After all, children deserve to have a special place to go when they don't want to be bothered; hence the chair's name. (As mothers, Judy and I wouldn't mind having "Don't Bug Me!" chairs of our own!)

Grass painting

Seat

7. Repeat steps 5 and 6 to mix Evergreen, extender, and water; then paint the Evergreen blades of grass.
8. Stencil the designs. Refer to the photos as necessary and to the "Stencil Color Guide" provided below. For detailed stenciling instructions, see "Stenciling" on pages 13–15. Here's one tip: Position the stenciled letters on the back slats at different angles to achieve a childlike look.

9. Sign your chair and allow all the paint to dry for several days. Then protect your work by applying at least 3 coats of varnish. (See "Final Touches" on page 19.)
10. For optional accessorizing, tie a bug net to one of the back legs with raffia.

STENCIL COLOR GUIDE

CHAIR PARTS	STENCILS	COLORS
Back slats	"Don't Bug Me!" from Complete Alphabet	Khaki Tan, Easy Blend Charcoal Grey
Other chair parts	Dragonflies from Whimsy Critters	Metallic Green Pearl, Metallic Ice Blue, Black, Olive Green
	Ladybugs from Whimsy Critters	Black, Tomato Red, Moon Yellow, Marigold
	Ants from Garden Critters	Black
	Caterpillar from Garden Critters	Hauser Light Green, Hauser Medium Green
	Butterfly from Butterflies	Black, Violet Haze
	Bees from Creepy Crawlers	Marigold, Black, Easy Blend Charcoal Grey
	Spiders and beetles from Creepy Crawlers	Black, Soft Black, Charcoal Grey, Santa Red

BEE HAPPY

TOOLS AND SUPPLIES

Required tools and supplies (see pages 6–8)

Embossing tool

Acrylic paints

To reproduce the photographed chair, use the DecoArt Americana paints listed below, or substitute other acrylic paints for a different look.

Soft Sage (DA207)—2 bottles

Jade Green (DA57)

Violet Haze (DA197)

Camel (DA191)

Honey Brown (DA163)

Black (DA67)

Taffy Cream (DA05)

Marigold (DA194)

Asphaltum (DA180)

Easy Blend Charcoal Grey (DEB28)

White (DA01)

Stencils

If you'd like to reproduce this chair exactly as it's shown, use the Stencilled Garden stencils listed here; they're available at specialty stencil stores and through mail-order suppliers. (See "Suppliers" on page 95.) For a different look, just substitute other stencils.

Honey Pot (TSG193)

Complete Alphabet (TSG810)

~~Ashley's Tea Party (TSG183)~~ *use girly's flowers*

Buzzy Bee Border (TSG825)

Checkerboards (TSG706)

INSTRUCTIONS

1. Prepare your chair for painting. (See "Chair Preparation" on pages 11–12.)

2. Apply as many base coats as necessary to achieve smooth, opaque coverage on the entire chair. (See "Base-Coat Painting" on page 12.) For correct color placement, refer to the photos and to the "Base-Coat Color Guide" provided below.

3. Stencil the designs. Refer to the photos as necessary and to the "Stencil Color Guide" provided on page 34. For detailed stenciling instructions, see "Stenciling" on pages 13–15.

Top back slat, front view

BASE-COAT COLOR GUIDE

CHAIR PARTS	COLORS
Top back slat, chair arms, tray, seat	Soft Sage
Tray arms, footrest	Jade Green
Legs	Jade Green, Soft Sage, Violet Haze
Back spindles	Jade Green, Violet Haze, Soft Sage
Stretchers	Jade Green, Violet Haze, Soft Sage

*J*udy had looked for a high chair for years, but her hunt intensified when she found out that her daughter was expecting her first baby. Unfortunately, several months of searching failed to uncover one, so off we went to the unfinished-furniture store. Judy was very happy; she not only found a high chair but one in the style she wanted (the tray lifts up and over the baby). She designed this project for her granddaughter, Samantha; we know Samantha will enjoy playing with the "bees."

Top back slat, back view

Tray top

4. Using an embossing tool, apply Soft Sage La De Da Dots to the centers of the flowers on the top back slat and tray top. (See "La De Da Dots" on page 18.)

5. Sign your chair and allow all the paint to dry for several days. Then protect your work by applying at least 3 coats of varnish. (See "Final Touches" on page 19.)

STENCIL COLOR GUIDE

CHAIR PARTS	STENCILS	COLORS
Top back slat	Beeskep from Honey Pot	Camel, Honey Brown, Black, Taffy Cream, Marigold, Asphaltum, Easy Blend Charcoal Grey
	"Bee Happy" from Complete Alphabet	Violet Haze
	Bees from Honey Pot, placed randomly	Camel, Honey Brown, Black, Taffy Cream, Marigold, Easy Blend Charcoal Grey
	Flowers from Ashley's Tea Party, placed randomly	Violet Haze, Jade Green, Soft Sage
Tray top	Beeskep from Buzzy Bee Border	Camel, Honey Brown, Black, Taffy Cream, Marigold, Asphaltum, Easy Blend Charcoal Grey
	Bees from Buzzy Bee Border, placed randomly	Camel, Honey Brown, Black, Taffy Cream, Marigold, Easy Blend Charcoal Grey
	Flowers from Ashley's Tea Party, placed randomly	Violet Haze, Jade Green, Soft Sage
Outer edge of tray	Checkerboards: ¾"	White, Black

SUGAR, SPICE, AND EVERYTHING NICE

TOOLS AND SUPPLIES

Required tools and supplies (see pages 6–8)
Transparent graph ruler
Watercolor pencil—any light color
Embossing tool
Acrylic paints

To reproduce the photographed chair, use the DecoArt Americana paints listed below, or substitute other acrylic paints for a different look.

Wisteria (DA211)—2 bottles
Deep Periwinkle (DA212)
French Vanilla (DA184)
Buttermilk (DA03)
Moon Yellow (DA07)
Easy Blend Charcoal Grey (DEB28)
Black (DA67)
Hauser Medium Green (DA132)

Stencils

If you'd like to reproduce this chair exactly as it's shown, use the Stencilled Garden stencils listed here; they're available at specialty stencil stores and through mail-order suppliers. (See "Suppliers" on page 95.) For a different look, just substitute other stencils.

Small Classic Bow Border (TSG150)
Buggy Border (TSG827)

INSTRUCTIONS

1. Prepare your chair for painting. (See "Chair Preparation" on pages 11–12.)
2. Apply as many base coats as necessary to achieve smooth, opaque coverage on the entire chair. (See "Base-Coat Painting" on page 12.) For correct color placement, refer to the photos and to the "Base-Coat Color Guide" provided below.
3. Using your transparent graph ruler and watercolor pencil, mark a 3" diamond pattern on the seat, as shown in the photos.
4. Before painting the lines you've just marked, press strips of removable painter's tape along the 2 outer edges of each line. Leave $1/8$"-wide gaps between the pieces of tape. Burnish the edges of the tape; then paint the $1/8$"-wide gaps with French Vanilla. (See "Stripes" on pages 17–18.) Allow the paint to dry and remove the strips of tape.
5. Stencil the designs. Refer to the photos as necessary and to the "Stencil Color Guide" provided on page 37. For detailed stenciling instructions, see "Stenciling" on pages 13–15.

BASE-COAT COLOR GUIDE

CHAIR PARTS	COLORS
Top back slat, seat	Wisteria
Back spindles	Wisteria, Deep Periwinkle
Legs (top to bottom)	Wisteria, French Vanilla, Deep Periwinkle, French Vanilla, Wisteria, French Vanilla, Deep Periwinkle
Stretchers	Deep Periwinkle

Judy asked her grandson, Josh, to join her for a special day of chair-hunting, so off they went to an antiques and collectibles show. There, Josh proved himself to be an excellent chair hunter. Not only did he find this chair (a perfect one for our book), but he also discovered two more, which Judy immediately bought and took home.

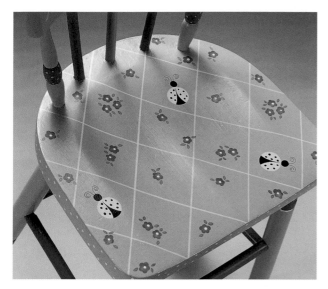

Seat

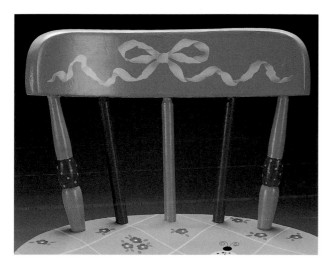

Top back slat, front view

6. Using an embossing tool, apply French Vanilla La De Da Dots along the edges of the seat and on the outermost back spindles, as shown in the photos. (See "La De Da Dots" on page 18.)

La De Da Dots on edge of seat

7. Sign your chair and allow all the paint to dry for several days. Then protect your work by applying at least 3 coats of varnish. (See "Final Touches" on page 19.)

STENCIL COLOR GUIDE

CHAIR PARTS	STENCILS	COLORS
Top back slat	Small Classic Bow Border	Buttermilk, French Vanilla, Moon Yellow, Easy Blend Charcoal Grey
Seat	Ladybugs and flowers from Buggy Border, placed randomly	French Vanilla, Black, Deep Periwinkle, Hauser Medium Green

*T*he unusual style of this chair inspired the animal print motif. With all the wonderful colors that we've been seeing in fabrics and accessories lately, we also decided to use a unique color palette. We painted the chair first, and then we went hunting for fabric. Judy and I both fell in love with the gold-striped material we found; it provided another great way to mix patterns on this chair.

ANIMAL FRENZY

TOOLS AND SUPPLIES

Required tools and supplies (see pages 6–8)
Screwdriver
Fabric for seat
Fabric painting medium
Repositionable spray adhesive
Sheet of smooth cardboard
Press cloth
Iron
Acrylic paints

> *To reproduce the photographed chair, use the DecoArt Americana paints listed below, or substitute other acrylic paints for a different look.*

Reindeer Moss Green (DA187)
Black (DA67)
Deep Burgundy (DA128)
Gooseberry Pink (DA27)
Violet Haze (DA197)
Raw Sienna (DA93)
Burnt Umber (DA64)
Buttermilk (DA03)
Camel (DA191)

Stencils

> *If you'd like to reproduce this chair exactly as it's shown, use the Stencilled Garden stencils listed here; they're available at specialty stencil stores and through mail-order suppliers.*

(See "Suppliers" on page 95.) For a different look, just substitute other stencils.
Giraffe Print (TSG230)
Zebra Print (TSG129)
Animal Print (TSG127)
Wild Animal Print (TSG128)
Jubee's Cow Print (TSG231)

INSTRUCTIONS

1. Remove the seat from your chair and set it aside.
2. Prepare your chair for painting. (See "Chair Preparation" on pages 11–12.)
3. Apply as many base coats as necessary to achieve smooth, opaque coverage on the entire chair. (See "Base-Coat Painting" on page 12.) For correct color placement, refer to the photos and to the "Base-Coat Color Guide" provided below.
4. Stencil the designs. Refer to the photos as necessary and to the "Stencil Color Guide" provided on the next page. For detailed stenciling instructions, see "Stenciling" on pages 13–15.

BASE-COAT COLOR GUIDE

CHAIR PARTS	COLORS
Top back slat, side stretchers	Reindeer Moss Green
Center back slat	Black
Back legs, center stretcher	Deep Burgundy
Skirt rail	Gooseberry Pink
Front legs	Violet Haze

Side and center stretchers

Skirt rail

Back slats

5. Prepare your new fabric for painting. (See "Stenciling on Fabric" on page 15.)

6. On your palette, mix 2 parts Black paint with 1 part fabric painting medium. Stencil the new fabric with this mixture, using the Jubee's Cow Print stencil. When the paint has dried, remove the stencil and use a press cloth and iron to heat-set the paint.

7. Sign your chair and allow all the paint to dry for several days. Then protect your work by applying at least 3 coats of varnish. (See "Final Touches" on page 19.)

8. Take the chair, your stenciled fabric, and the old seat to an upholsterer who can make a new seat, attach your fabric to it, and attach the seat to the chair. (See "Final Touches" on page 19.)

STENCIL COLOR GUIDE

CHAIR PARTS	STENCILS	COLORS
Top back slat	Giraffe Print	Raw Sienna, Burnt Umber
Outer edge of each back leg	Zebra Print	Black
Skirt rails	Animal Print	Black, Buttermilk, Camel
Front legs	Wild Animal Print	Black

HOME RUN

TOOLS AND SUPPLIES

Required tools and supplies (see pages 6–8)
Faux glazing medium
Natural sea wool sponge
Acrylic paints

To reproduce the photographed chair, use the DecoArt Americana paints listed below, or substitute other acrylic paints for a different look.

Camel (DA191)
Black (DA67)
Shale Green (DA152)
Buttermilk (DA03)
Honey Brown (DA163)
White (DA01)
Country Red (DA18)
Burnt Umber (DA64)
Asphaltum (DA180)

Stencils

If you'd like to reproduce this chair exactly as it's shown, use the Stencilled Garden stencils listed here; they're available at specialty stencil stores and through mail-order suppliers. (See "Suppliers" on page 95.) For a different look, just substitute other stencils.

Wild Animal Print (TSG128)
Lil Checks (TSG707)
Zebra Print (TSG129)
Play Ball (TSG185)
A Fielder's Dream (TSG804)

INSTRUCTIONS

1. Prepare your chair for painting. (See "Chair Preparation" on pages 11–12.)
2. Apply as many base coats as necessary to achieve smooth, opaque coverage on the entire chair. (See "Base-Coat Painting" on page 12.) For correct color placement, refer to the photos and to the "Base-Coat Color Guide" provided below.
3. Using removable painter's tape, mask off all chair parts that are adjacent to the areas painted with Camel.
4. On your palette, mix 1 part Honey Brown paint with 3 parts faux glazing medium. Then, with your sea wool sponge, lightly sponge all the Camel-painted areas with the glaze mixture. (See "Sponged Faux Finishes" on page 16.)
5. Stencil the designs. Refer to the photos as necessary and to the "Stencil Color Guide" provided on page 43. For detailed stenciling instructions, see "Stenciling" on pages 13–15.

Top back slat

BASE-COAT COLOR GUIDE

CHAIR PARTS	COLORS
Top and bottom back slats, back stretcher, front legs	Camel
Back legs, front stretcher	Black
Outer back slats, seat, 2 side stretchers	Shale Green
Center back slat, 2 side stretchers	Buttermilk

Years ago, I decided to find and paint four different chairs for my dining room—one to fit each family member's personality. This is my son Tyler's chair. His love of baseball was the main focus of the design, but he also decided that he wanted an animal print on his chair. For easy cleanup, I chose chairs with wooden seats for both Tyler and my daughter.

Outer edge of back leg

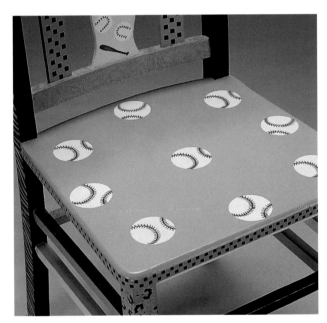

Seat

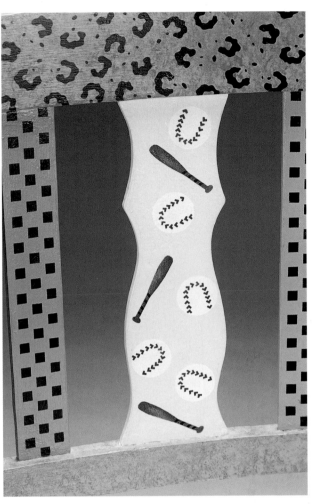

Center and outer back slats

6. Sign your chair and allow all the paint to dry for several days. Then protect your work by applying at least 3 coats of varnish. (See "Final Touches" on page 19.)

STENCIL COLOR GUIDE

CHAIR PARTS	STENCILS	COLORS
Top back slat, front legs	Wild Animal Print	Black
Outer back slats, edges of seat	Lil Checks	Black
Outer edges of back legs	Zebra Print	White
Center back slat (front and rear)	Play Ball	White, Country Red, Burnt Umber, Asphaltum, Black
Top of seat	A Fielder's Dream	White, Country Red

*I*n the same way I that designed the "Home Run" dining-room chair (see page 42) for my son, I decorated this dining-room chair for my daughter, Ashley. She and I devoted many hours to picking out the stencil patterns and colors. What a wonderful time we had together, creating this special chair for a special girl.

MIXED BREED

TOOLS AND SUPPLIES

Required tools and supplies (see pages 6–8)
Transparent graph ruler
Watercolor pencil—light yellow
Embossing tool
Cotton swabs
Acrylic paints

To reproduce the photographed chair, use the DecoArt Americana paints listed below, or substitute other acrylic paints for a different look.

Black (DA67)
Light Buttermilk (DA164)
White (DA01)
Violet Haze (DA197)
Wisteria (DA211)
Olive Green (DA56)
French Mauve (DA186)
French Vanilla (DA184)
Napa Red (DA165)
Buttermilk (DA03)
Tomato Red (DA169)
Evergreen (DA82)
Camel (DA191)
Honey Brown (DA163)

Stencils

If you'd like to reproduce this chair exactly as it's shown, use the Stencilled Garden stencils listed here; they're available at specialty stencil stores and through mail-order suppliers. (See "Suppliers" on page 95.) For a different look, just substitute other stencils.

Cherries Jubilee (TSG184)
Animal Print (TSG127)
Checkerboards (TSG706)
Girly's Flower Border (TSG122)
Wild Animal Print (TSG128)

INSTRUCTIONS

1. Prepare your chair for painting. (See "Chair Preparation" on pages 11–12.)
2. Apply as many base coats as necessary to achieve smooth, opaque coverage on the entire chair. (See "Base-Coat Painting" on page 12.) For correct color placement, refer to the photos and to the "Base-Coat Color Guide" provided below.
3. Using your transparent graph ruler and watercolor pencil, mark 1"-wide stripes on the seat, as shown in the photos. Before

BASE-COAT COLOR GUIDE

CHAIR PARTS	COLORS
Top back slat	Black
Vertical back slat, seat	Light Buttermilk
Bottom back slat	White
1 back leg, 1 side stretcher	Violet Haze
1 back leg, 1 side stretcher	Wisteria
Skirt rails, center stretcher	Olive Green
Back stretcher	French Mauve
Front legs (top to bottom)	Black, Wisteria, French Vanilla, Napa Red, Violet Haze, French Mauve, Black, Olive Green

painting the stripes you've just marked, press strips of removable painter's tape along the 2 outer edges of each one, leaving 1"-wide gaps between the pieces of tape. Burnish the edges of the tape. (See "Stripes" on pages 17–18.)

4. To color the stripes, apply a Buttermilk color wash to them. (See "Color Washing" on pages 15–16.) Allow the paint to dry and remove the strips of tape.

5. Stencil the designs. Refer to the photos as necessary and to the "Stencil Color Guide" provided below. For detailed stenciling instructions, see "Stenciling" on pages 13–15. Here's a tip: Stencil the top back slat with White paint and let it dry before you apply the other stencil colors. If you apply your colors directly on top of the Black base coats, they won't show.

Seat

Top back slat

Skirt rail

6. Using an embossing tool, apply Black La De Da Dots to the seat top and White La De Da Dots to the legs and top back slat. (See "La De Da Dots" on page 18.) For correct placement, refer to the photos.

7. Sign your chair and allow all the paint to dry for several days. Then protect your work by applying at least 3 coats of varnish. (See "Final Touches" on page 19.)

STENCIL COLOR GUIDE

CHAIR PARTS	STENCILS	COLORS
Top back slat	Cherries Jubilee	White, Tomato Red, Napa Red, Evergreen
Vertical back slat	Animal Print	Camel, Honey Brown, Black
Bottom back slat	Checkerboards: ¾"	Black
Top of seat	Flowers from Girly's Flower Border, placed randomly	Wisteria, Violet Haze, Olive Green, Evergreen
Skirt rails	Wild Animal Print	Black

BUZZY BEE

TOOLS AND SUPPLIES

Required tools and supplies (see pages 6–8)
Empty 2-ounce bottle with lid
Embossing tool
Cotton swabs
Acrylic paints

To reproduce the photographed chair, use the DecoArt Americana paints listed below, or substitute other acrylic paints for a different look.

Country Blue (DA41)
White (DA01)
Sand (DA04)
Black (DA67)
Camel (DA191)
Honey Brown (DA163)
Evergreen (DA82)
Light Buttermilk (DA164)
Marigold (DA194)
Easy Blend Charcoal Grey (DEB28)

Stencils

If you'd like to reproduce this chair exactly as it's shown, use the Stencilled Garden stencils listed here; they're available at specialty stencil stores and through mail-order suppliers. (See "Suppliers" on page 95.) For a different look, just substitute other stencils.

Buzzy Beeskep (TSG826)
Wild Posies (TSG190)
Buzzy Bee Border (TSG825)
Lil Checks (TSG707)

INSTRUCTIONS

1. Prepare your chair for painting. (See "Chair Preparation" on pages 11–12.)
2. The base-coat color on this chair is a mixture of Country Blue and White. Start by filling four-fifths of an empty 2-ounce bottle with White paint. Then add Country Blue to create a very pale blue, shaking the mixture well. (Acrylic colors are darker when they're dry than they are in their bottles. To test a color, brush some of the paint onto a piece of paper and let it dry.)
3. Apply as many base coats as necessary to achieve smooth, opaque coverage on the entire chair. (See "Base-Coat Painting" on page 12.) For correct color placement, refer to the photos and to the "Base-Coat Color Guide" provided below.
4. Stencil the designs. Refer to the photos as necessary and to the "Stencil Color Guide" provided on page 49. For detailed stenciling instructions, see "Stenciling" on pages 13–15.

BASE-COAT COLOR GUIDE

CHAIR PARTS	COLORS
Top and bottom back slats	Country Blue/White
Side stretchers (1 end to the other)	Country Blue/White, Sand, Country Blue/White
Center stretcher (1 end to the other)	Black, County Blue/White, Black
Center back slat, seat, back stretcher	Sand
Back legs	Black
Front legs (top to bottom)	Black, Country Blue/White, Black, Country Blue/White, Sand, Black

Judy and I found this chair on one of many chair-hunting trips. We purchased two chairs from a set of six, but after we painted this one, we wished we'd bought the other four, too. Oops! Now, when we find a set of chairs, we think long and hard before leaving any of them behind.

Side and center stretchers

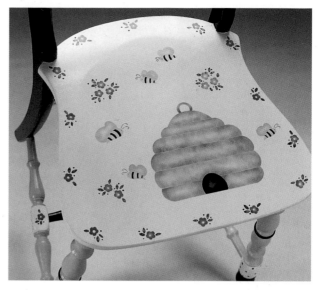

Seat

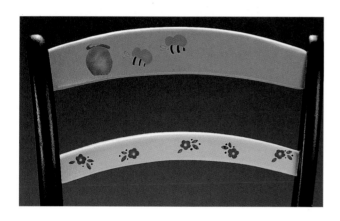

Back slats, front view

5. Using an embossing tool, apply Black La De Da Dots around each flower. (See "La De Da Dots" on page 18.) Use cotton swabs to apply Black La De Da Dots on the front legs. For correct placement, refer to the photos.

6. Sign your chair and allow all the paint to dry for several days. Then protect your work by applying at least 3 coats of varnish. (See "Final Touches" on page 19.)

STENCIL COLOR GUIDE

CHAIR PARTS	STENCILS	COLORS
Seat	Beeskep from Buzzy Beeskep	Camel, Honey Brown, Black
	Flowers from Wild Posies, placed randomly	Country Blue/White, Evergreen, Light Buttermilk
Top back slat	Honey pot and bees from Buzzy Bee Border	Camel, Honey Brown, Sand, Marigold, Black, Easy Blend Charcoal Grey
Center back slat	Flowers from Wild Posies, placed randomly	Country Blue/White, Evergreen, Light Buttermilk
Back stretcher	Lil Checks	Black
Centers of side stretchers	Flowers from Wild Posies, placed randomly	Country Blue/White, Evergreen, Light Buttermilk

When we found this chair, it definitely looked like it belonged at the beach, so we designed it to look as if it were already there. We now own several of these solid-backed chairs; we thought we had to buy every one we found!

BEACH TIME

TOOLS AND SUPPLIES

Required tools and supplies (see pages 6–8)
Faux glazing medium
Natural sea wool sponge
Acrylic paints

To reproduce the photographed chair, use the DecoArt Americana paints listed below, or substitute other acrylic paints for a different look.

Sand (DA04)—2 bottles
Antique White (DA58)
Desert Sand (DA77)
Winter Blue (DA190)
White (DA01)
Admiral Blue (DA213)
Khaki Tan (DA173)
Taffy Cream (DA05)
Olive Green (DA56)
Hauser Light Green (DA131)
Black (DA67)
Country Red (DA18)
Easy Blend Charcoal Grey (DEB28)

Stencil

If you'd like to reproduce this chair exactly as it's shown, use the Stencilled Garden stencil listed here; it's available at specialty stencil stores and through mail-order suppliers. (See "Suppliers" on page 95.) For a different look, just substitute a different stencil.

Day at the Beach (TSG830)

INSTRUCTIONS

1. Prepare your chair for painting. (See "Chair Preparation" on pages 11–12.)
2. Using the Sand paint, apply as many base coats as necessary to achieve smooth, opaque coverage on the entire chair. (See "Base-Coat Painting" on page 12.)
3. Using removable painter's tape, mask the lower portion of the area that will become the ocean.
4. On your palette, mix 1 part Antique White paint with 3 parts faux glazing medium. Then create the "sand" by using your natural sea wool sponge and the glaze mixture to sponge all portions of the chair below the tape. (See "Sponged Faux Finishes" on page 16.)
5. Repeat step 4 to sponge a mixture of 1 part Desert Sand paint and 3 parts faux glazing medium over the same portions of the chair. When the paint has dried, remove the tape.
6. Position 2 new pieces of tape on the chair: 1 to mask off the very top of the "sand" you just sponged and another approximately 2½" to 3" above the first. The exposed area between the 2 pieces of tape will become the ocean.
7. Using diluted Winter Blue, apply a color wash to the ocean, starting with a dark shade at the top and fading down to a lighter shade at the bottom. (See "Color Washing" on pages 15–16.) Allow the wash to dry. When the paint has dried, remove the tape.
8. Place a new piece of tape across the top edge of the ocean area to protect the Winter Blue wash. Prepare a very pale Winter Blue wash for the sky and apply it to all portions of the chair above the tape. Allow the wash to dry and remove the tape.
9. Stencil the designs from the Day at the Beach stencil with the following colors: White, Admiral Blue, Khaki Tan, Taffy Cream, Olive Green, Hauser Light Green, Black, Country Red, and Easy Blend Charcoal Grey. (See "Stenciling" on pages 13–15). Use the photo as a guide to design placement and colors.

10. To create the edges of the sand dunes and the white caps on the ocean waves, use a ½"-wide flat artist's brush to stipple the paints onto the chair. Use Antique White and White for the sand dunes and White for the white caps. Here's a tip: To help make the stenciled beach items look as if they're sitting in the sand, layer some of the sand dune edges over the bottom edges of the beach items.

11. Sign your chair and allow the paint to dry for several days. Then protect your work by applying at least 3 coats of varnish. (See "Final Touches" on page 19.)

Folded chair from front

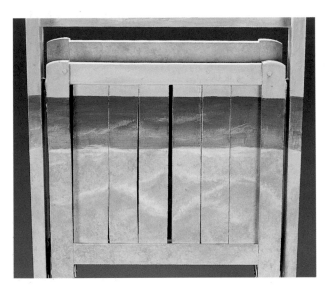

Folded chair

Chair back, front view

Seat

FARMER'S MARKET

TOOLS AND SUPPLIES

Required tools and supplies (see pages 6–8)
Crackle medium
Acrylic paints

To reproduce the photographed chair, use the DecoArt Americana paints listed below, or substitute other acrylic paints for a different look.

French Vanilla (DA184)—2 to 3 bottles
Moon Yellow (DA07)
Prussian Blue (DA138)
Payne's Grey (DA167)
Country Blue (DA41)
Plantation Pine (DA113)
Celery Green (DA208)
Asphaltum (DA180)
White (DA01)
Plum (DA175)
Black Plum (DA172)
Hauser Light Green (DA131)
Royal Purple (DA150)
Pansy Lavender (DA154)
Evergreen (DA82)
Peach Sherbert (DA217)
Shading Flesh (DA137)
Burnt Sienna (DA63)

Stencils

If you'd like to reproduce this chair exactly as it's shown, use the Stencilled Garden stencils listed here; they're available at specialty stencil stores and through mail-order suppliers. (See "Suppliers" on page 95.) For a different look, just substitute other stencils.
Checkerboards (TSG706)
Complete Alphabet (TSG810)
Blueberry Vine (TSG406)
Farmer's Market (TSG414)

INSTRUCTIONS

1. Prepare your chair for painting. (See "Chair Preparation" on pages 11–12.)
2. Using French Vanilla, apply as many base coats as necessary to achieve smooth, opaque coverage over the entire chair. (See "Base-Coat Painting" on page 12.)
3. Apply crackle medium randomly to the top back slat, seat, and legs. (See "Crackle Finishes" on page 17.) Allow the medium to dry completely; then apply a French Vanilla topcoat.
4. Paint 2 of the back slats and the rings on the legs with 2 coats of Moon Yellow. For correct color placement, refer to the photos.
5. Stencil the designs. Refer to the photos as necessary and to the "Stencil Color Guide" provided on page 55. For detailed stenciling instructions, see "Stenciling" on pages 13–15. Here's a tip: When stenciling the Blueberry Vine, "free-form" the design by moving the stencil to wrap the vine over and around the words "Farmer's Market."

Top back slat, front view

A friend of ours told us about an antique shop she'd discovered. Although it took us several hours to drive there, the trip was worth it. We retrieved this chair from the shop's rafters, and after blowing off the dust that had accumulated over many years, found the perfect chair for my kitchen desk. After hours of sanding off the old finish, we decided that the chair would never be perfect, so I chose an antiqued and distressed finish for it.

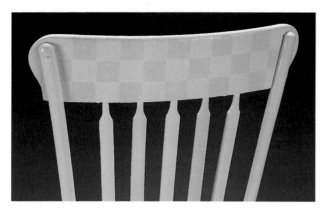

Top back slat, rear view

Stenciled peach on seat

Stenciled plum on seat

Stenciled damson on seat

6. Sign your chair and allow all the paint to dry for several days. Then protect your work by applying at least 3 coats of varnish. (See "Final Touches" on page 19.)

STENCIL COLOR GUIDE

CHAIR PARTS	STENCILS	COLORS
Top back slat	Checkerboards: 1½"	Moon Yellow
	"Farmer's Market" from Complete Alphabet	Prussian Blue, Payne's Grey
	Blueberry Vine	Country Blue, Prussian Blue, Payne's Grey, Plantation Pine, Celery Green, Asphaltum, White
Top of seat	Checkerboards: 1½"	Moon Yellow
	Fruits from Farmer's Market, placed randomly	White, Asphaltum, Plum, Black Plum, Hauser Light Green, Royal Purple, Pansy Lavender, Payne's Grey, Evergreen, Peach Sherbert, Shading Flesh, Burnt Sienna

*I*nspired by a chair that a friend in Pennsylvania painted, we set out to search for a similar chair. We were surprised to find, at an unfinished furniture store, a chair that looked as much like our friend's as this one does.

HARLEQUIN

TOOLS AND SUPPLIES

Required tools and supplies (see pages 6–8)
Faux glazing medium
Natural sea wool sponge
#1 liner brush
Embossing tool
Acrylic paints

> *To reproduce the photographed chair, use the DecoArt Americana paints listed below, or substitute other acrylic paints for a different look.*

   Moon Yellow (DA07)
   Tomato Red (DA169)
   White (DA01)—2 to 3 bottles
   Black (DA67)
   Prussian Blue (DA138)
   Peony Pink (DA215)
   Blue Violet (DA141)
   Payne's Grey (DA167)
   Cranberry Wine (DA112)
   Easy Blend Charcoal Grey (DEB28)

Stencils

> *If you'd like to reproduce this chair exactly as it's shown, use the Stencilled Garden stencils listed here; they're available at specialty stencil stores and through mail-order suppliers. (See "Suppliers" on page 95.) For a different look, just substitute other stencils.*

   Squiggles & Dots (TSG178)
   Lil Checks (TSG707)
   Diamonds Galore (TSG138)

INSTRUCTIONS

1. Prepare your chair for painting. (See "Chair Preparation" on pages 11–12.)
2. Apply as many base coats as necessary to achieve smooth, opaque coverage on the entire chair. (See "Base-Coat Painting" on page 12.) For correct color placement, refer to the photos and to the "Base-Coat Color Guide" provided on the next page.
3. Using removable painter's tape, mask all portions of the chair that are adjacent to those that will be marbleized. (As you can see in the photos, the marbleized areas are greyish blue.)
4. On your palette, mix 1 part Prussian Blue with 3 parts faux glazing medium. Also mix 1 part Payne's Grey with 3 parts faux glazing medium. To create a marbleized finish, you'll start by applying 4 or 5 sponged glaze coats, alternating the 2 different colors. If you like, occasionally mix the 2 colors by applying one while the other is still wet. Then, using your sea wool sponge, lightly sponge all the areas that you painted with White, except for the seat, middle back slat, and uppermost portion of the vertical arms. (See "Marbleized Finishes" on page 17.)
5. To create the veins on the marbleized areas, use a #1 liner brush to apply jagged and curved lines of Payne's Grey paint mixed with glaze.
6. Mix 1 part Cranberry Wine and 3 parts faux glazing medium on your palette. Use an artist's brush to apply it over all the areas painted with Peony Pink.

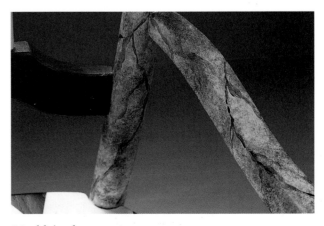

Marbleized armrest

BASE-COAT COLOR GUIDE

CHAIR PARTS	COLORS
Back legs (top to bottom)	Moon Yellow, Tomato Red, White, Black
Top back slat	Prussian Blue
Center back slat, seat, horizontal arms	White
Fan-shaped back slats	Moon Yellow
Bottom back slat, upper side stretchers	Peony Pink
Lower side stretchers (one end to the other)	White, Tomato Red, White
Upper back stretcher	Peony Pink
Lower back stretcher	Blue Violet
Vertical arms (top to bottom)	White, Tomato Red, Black, Moon Yellow, Black, White, Moon Yellow, Prussian Blue
Center stretcher (one end to the other)	White, Prussian Blue, Peony Pink, Prussian Blue, White
Front skirt rail	Blue Violet
Front legs (top to bottom)	Black, Moon Yellow, Black, Tomato Red, Black, Moon Yellow, Peony Pink, Black

7. Stencil the designs. Refer to the photo as necessary and to the "Stencil Color Guide" provided below. For detailed stenciling instructions, see "Stenciling" on pages 13–15. Here's one tip before you begin: To create the shadow effect around each of the diamonds on the seat, first stencil the diamonds with Black and the circles that connect them with Blue Violet. When the stenciled diamonds and circles have dried, shift the stencil so that its open portions now rest over the diamond-shaped areas that you haven't stenciled. Using Easy Blend Charcoal Grey, lightly stencil around the edges of the stencil windows; these stenciled lines will rest along the outer edges of the diamonds you've already stenciled. (Alternatively, remove the stencil; then use a $\frac{1}{4}$"-wide artist's brush for freehand application of the Easy Blend Charcoal Grey.)

8. Using the photo as a placement guide and an embossing tool as an applicator, paint White La De Da Dots on the legs and Black La De Da Dots on the legs and vertical arms. (See "La De Da Dots" on page 18.)

9. Sign your chair and allow all the paint to dry for several days. Then protect your work by applying at least 3 coats of varnish. (See "Final Touches" on page 19.)

STENCIL COLOR GUIDE

CHAIR PARTS	STENCILS	COLORS
Top back slat	Squiggles & Dots	White
Narrow center back slat	Lil Checks	Black
Seat	Diamonds Galore	Black, Blue Violet, Easy Blend Charcoal Grey

CHERRIES JUBILEE

TOOLS AND SUPPLIES

Required tools and supplies (see pages 6–8)
Empty 2-ounce bottle with lid
Embossing tool
Fabric for seat and back
Fabric painting medium
Sheet of smooth cardboard
Repositionable spray adhesive
Press cloth
Iron
Acrylic paints

To reproduce the photographed chair, use the DecoArt Americana paints listed below, or substitute other acrylic paints for a different look.

Country Blue (DA41)
White (DA01)
Tomato Red (DA169)
Black (DA67)
Marigold (DA194)
Evergreen (DA82)

Stencils

If you'd like to reproduce this chair exactly as it's shown, use the Stencilled Garden stencils listed here; they're available at specialty stencil stores and through mail-order suppliers. (See "Suppliers" on page 95.) For a different look, just substitute other stencils.

Wild Posies (TSG190)
Checkerboards (TSG706)
Double Checks (TSG713-2)
Cherry Pickin' (TSG709S)

INSTRUCTIONS

1. Take the chair to an upholsterer for removal of the seat and back.
2. Prepare the chair for painting. (See "Chair Preparation" on pages 11–12.)
3. One of the base-coat colors on this chair is a mixture of Country Blue and White. To mix this color, start by filling four-fifths of your empty 2-ounce bottle with White paint. Then add Country Blue paint to create a very pale blue, shaking the mixture well. (Acrylic colors are darker when they're dry than they are in their bottles. To test the color, brush some of the paint onto a piece of paper and let it dry.)
4. Apply as many base coats as necessary to achieve smooth, opaque coverage on the entire chair. (See "Base-Coat Painting" on page 12.) For correct color placement, refer to the photos and to the "Base-Coat Color Guide" provided below.
5. Stencil the designs. Refer to the photos as necessary and to the "Stencil Color Guide" provided on page 61. For detailed stenciling instructions, see "Stenciling" on pages 13–15.
6. With an embossing tool, apply Country Blue/White La De Da Dots and Black La De Da Dots to the front legs. (See "La De Da Dots" on page 18.) For correct placement, refer to the photos.

BASE-COAT COLOR GUIDE

CHAIR PARTS	COLORS
Side stretchers	White
Arms, back legs	Country Blue/White
Front legs (top to bottom)	Tomato Red, White, Black, Country Blue/White, Black, White, Black, Country Blue/White, Tomato Red, Country Blue/White

I was lucky enough to receive this chair from a neighbor. Because there wasn't much wood to paint, I decided to stencil new fabric with my favorite designs. The chair now sits in a bay-window area in the living room of my new house, but I'm still hunting for a table and another chair to go with it.

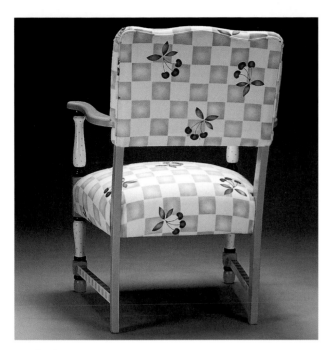

Back view

Front leg

7. Sign your chair and allow the paint to dry for several days. (Complete steps 8 through 10 while you wait.) Then protect your work by applying at least 3 coats of varnish. (See "Final Touches" on page 19.)

8. Prepare your new fabric for painting. (See "Stenciling on Fabric" on page 15.)

9. On your palette, mix 2 parts Country Blue/White with 1 part fabric painting medium. Stencil the new fabric with this mixture and the Double Checks stencil in an all-over repeat pattern.

10. Mix 2 parts Tomato Red with 1 part fabric painting medium. Using the Cherry Pickin' stencil, stencil the cherries onto the fabric. Then mix 2 parts Evergreen paint with 1 part fabric painting medium, and stencil the cherry leaves and stems. When the paint has dried, remove the stencil and use a press cloth and iron to heat-set the paint.

Fabric on chair back

11. Take the painted chair and your stenciled fabric to your upholstery shop. The upholsterer can make a new seat and back, and cover them with your fabric. (See "Final Touches" on page 19.)

STENCIL COLOR GUIDE

CHAIR PARTS	STENCILS	COLORS
Front legs	Flowers from Wild Posies, placed randomly	Marigold, Evergreen
Side stretchers	Checkerboards: ¾"	Country Blue/White

This chair, which Judy found during one of her trips, still had the manufacturer's original tag from the 1950s attached to its seat. I fell in love with the chair's style and added it my dining-room chair collection. When we have company, I now have at least one extra chair for a guest. I still need a few more to paint, though!

J'RENEE'S STYLE

TOOLS AND SUPPLIES

Required tools and supplies (see pages 6–8)
Faux glazing medium
Natural sea wool sponge
#1 liner brush
Embossing tool
Cotton swabs
Acrylic paints

> To reproduce the photographed chair, use the DecoArt Americana paints listed below, or substitute other acrylic paints for a different look.

Taffy Cream (DA05)
Light Buttermilk (DA164)
White (DA01)
Raspberry (DA28)
Reindeer Moss Green (DA187)
Winter Blue (DA190)
Black (DA67)
Celery Green (DA208)
Soft Black (DA155)
Summer Lilac (DA189)
Pansy Lavender (DA154)
Evergreen (DA82)

Stencils

> If you'd like to reproduce this chair exactly as it's shown, use the Stencilled Garden stencils listed here; they're available at specialty stencil stores and through mail-order suppliers. (See "Suppliers" on page 95.) For a different look, just substitute other stencils.

Checkerboards (TSG706)
Lil Checks (TSG707)
Diamond Vines (TSG242)

INSTRUCTIONS

1. Prepare your chair for painting. (See "Chair Preparation" on pages 11–12.)

2. Apply as many base coats as necessary to achieve smooth, opaque coverage on the entire chair. (See "Base-Coat Painting" on page 12.) For correct color placement, refer to the photos and to the "Base-Coat Color Guide" provided below.

3. Using removable painter's tape, mask off all areas adjacent to the back legs.

4. To marbleize the legs, start by mixing 1 part Taffy Cream paint with 3 parts faux glazing medium on your palette. Apply the paint with your natural sea wool sponge. Then mix 1 part Reindeer Moss Green with 3 parts faux glazing medium, and apply this coat with your sponge. Repeat to mix and apply a final coat of Celery Green paint and faux glazing medium. When the

BASE-COAT COLOR GUIDE

CHAIR PARTS	COLORS
Top back slat	Taffy Cream
Second and fourth back slats, seat	Light Buttermilk
Third back slat, front legs	White
Skirt rails	Raspberry
Back legs	Reindeer Moss Green
Side stretchers, back stretcher	Winter Blue
Center stretcher	Black

paint has dried, use your #1 liner brush to paint the marbleized lines with Soft Black mixed with glaze. (See "Marbleized Finishes" on page 17.)

5. Stencil the designs. Refer to the photos as necessary and to the "Stencil Color Guide" provided below. For detailed stenciling instructions, see "Stenciling" on pages 13–15.

Back slats

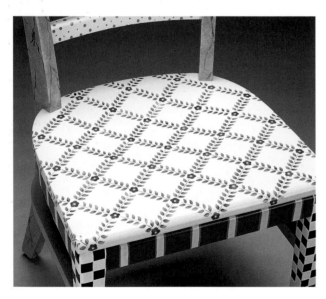

Seat

6. Paint the stripes on the skirt rails with a ¼"-wide flat artist's brush and Taffy Cream paint for the wide stripes, and a #1 liner brush and Summer Lilac for the narrow ones. If your freehand painting skills aren't the best, mark the stripes first, using a transparent graph ruler and a watercolor pencil. Then use removable painter's tape to mask adjacent areas before painting them. (See "Stripes" on pages 17–18.)

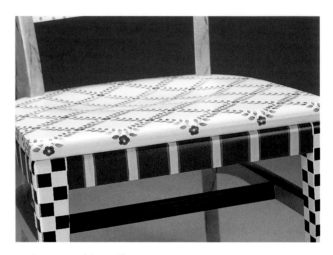

Stripes on skirt rail

7. Using an embossing tool, apply a Taffy Cream La De Da Dot to the center of each flower. (See "La De Da Dots" on page 18.) Use the same tool—and cotton swabs—to apply large and small Winter Blue La De Da Dots to the second and fourth back slats.

8. Sign your chair and allow the paint to dry for several days. Then protect your work by applying at least 3 coats of varnish. (See "Final Touches" on page 19.)

STENCIL COLOR GUIDE

CHAIR PARTS	STENCILS	COLORS
Top back slat	Checkerboards: 1"	Summer Lilac
Upper portion of front legs	Checkerboards: ¾"	Black
Bottom portion of front legs	Lil Checks	Black
Top of seat	Diamond Vines	Pansy Lavender, Evergreen
Third back slat	Flowers from Diamond Vines	Pansy Lavender

COBBLESTONE SQUARE

TOOLS AND SUPPLIES

Required tools and supplies (see pages 6–8)
Screwdriver
Empty 2-ounce bottle with lid
Gel stain (DS30)
Fabric for seat
Acrylic paints

> *To reproduce the photographed chair, use the DecoArt Americana paints listed below, or substitute other acrylic paints for a different look.*

> White (DA01)—2 bottles
> Reindeer Moss Green (DA187)
> Country Blue (DA41)
> Raw Umber (DA130)
> Charcoal Grey (DA88)
> Burnt Sienna (DA63)
> Burnt Umber (DA64)
> Light Avocado (DA106)
> Evergreen (DA82)
> Asphaltum (DA180)
> Khaki Tan (DA173)
> Driftwood (DA171)
> Plantation Pine (DA113)
> Easy Blend Charcoal Grey (DEB28)

Stencil

> *If you'd like to reproduce this chair exactly as it's shown, use the Stencilled Garden stencil listed here; it's available at specialty stencil stores and through mail-order suppliers. (See "Suppliers" on page 95.) For a different look, just substitute a different stencil.*
> Cobblestone Square (TSG906)

Back slat, front view

Back slat, back view

Front skirt rail

Inspired by the minimural stencil design Cobblestone Square, we set out in search of the perfect chair to go with it. And were we ever lucky! We discovered it in my neighbor's garage. She had five chairs that she no longer wanted. Sometimes you don't have to look very far for a chair; just let your friends and neighbors know that you're searching.

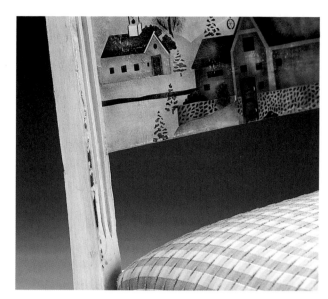

Bottom left corner of back slat

INSTRUCTIONS

1. Remove the seat from your chair and set it aside.
2. Prepare your chair for painting. (See "Chair Preparation" on pages 11–12.)
3. Apply as many White base coats as necessary to achieve smooth, opaque coverage on the entire chair. (See "Base-Coat Painting" on page 12.)
4. Using removable tape, mask all parts of the chair adjacent to the 3 skirt rails and upper portion of the top back slat.
5. With a 1"-wide stencil brush, stipple the skirt rails with Reindeer Moss Green.

Stippled surface

6. Fill four-fifths of your empty bottle with White paint. Add Country Blue to create a very pale blue, shaking the mixture well. (Acrylic colors are darker when they're dry than they are in their bottles. To test a color, brush some of the paint onto a piece of paper and let it dry.) Then use the mixed color to stipple the upper portion of the top back slat. When the stippled paint has dried, remove all the tape.
7. Using the Cobblestone Square stencil and all the colors listed for this project, stencil the wide back slat, placing half of the stenciled scene on the slat's front and the other half on the back. (See "Stenciling" on pages 13–15.) This stencil package specifies which colors to use in which areas of the design. Stipple the sky portion of the stencil design with the same Country Blue/White mixture that you used to stipple the upper portion of the top back slat.
8. On the front skirt rail, use Evergreen paint to stencil 3 small trees from the Cobblestone Square stencil.
9. Allow all the paint to dry for several days.
10. To create an antique, distressed look that will complement the stencil design, sand some areas of the chair down to the raw wood.
11. To create an antique faux finish, first use an artist's brush to apply 1 coat of varnish to the entire chair. Allow the varnish to dry. Then, working on one small area at a time, brush gel stain onto the chair and wipe it off. Continue until the entire chair is complete. (See "Antique Finishes" on page 16.)
12. Sign your chair and allow the paint to dry for several days. Then protect your work by applying at least 3 coats of varnish. (See "Final Touches" on page 19.)
13. Take the chair, your new fabric, and the old seat to an upholsterer, who can make a new seat, attach your fabric to it, and attach the seat to the chair. (See "Final Touches" on page 19.)

We found this chair at a local antique shop, complete with a metal tag that identified one of its previous owners as the Welfare Department. We removed the tag, cleaned it, and reattached it to the chair after we'd finished all the painting. The chair's simple style inspired our folk-art theme and whimsical style; we just had to add the wooden stars and birdhouse.

FOLK-ART BIRDHOUSE

TOOLS AND SUPPLIES

Required tools and supplies (see pages 6–8)
Empty 2-ounce bottle with lid
Faux glazing medium
Natural sea wool sponge
Wing, comb, or rake brush
Cotton swabs
Embossing tool
Black paint pen
Wood glue
Buttons
Wooden stars
Small birdhouse
Green moss
Wooden dowel, 1' long and 1" in diameter
Acrylic paints

To reproduce the photographed chair, use the DecoArt Americana paints listed below, or substitute other acrylic paints for a different look.

White Wash (DA02)
Antique White (DA58)
Forest Green (DA50)
Uniform Blue (DA86)
French Grey Blue (DA98)
Green Mist (DA177)
Antique Maroon (DA160)
Evergreen (DA82)
Burnt Umber (DA64)
Black (DA67)

Stencils

If you'd like to reproduce this chair exactly as it's shown, use the Stencilled Garden stencils listed here; they're available at specialty stencil stores and through mail-order suppliers. (See "Suppliers" on page 95.) For a different look, just substitute other stencils.

Let's Be a Star (TSG180)
Fresh Cherries (TSG223)
Fergie's Birdhouse Collection (TSG107)
Lil Checks (TSG707)

INSTRUCTIONS

1. Prepare your chair for painting. (See "Chair Preparation" on pages 11–12.)

2. Fill 70 percent of your empty bottle with White Wash paint and add Antique White until the bottle is full. Shake this mixture well; you'll use it in the next step.

3. Apply as many base coats as necessary to achieve smooth, opaque coverage on the entire chair. (See "Base-Coat Painting" on page 12.) For correct color placement, refer to the photos and to the "Base-Coat Color Guide" provided on page 70.

4. Using removable tape, cover the Antique Maroon borders around the top of the seat. Burnish the edges of the tape well.

5. On your palette, mix 1 part Antique White paint with 3 parts faux glazing medium. Then, using your natural sea wool sponge, lightly sponge the center of the seat. (See "Sponged Faux Finishes" on page 16.)

6. Stencil the designs. Refer to the photo as necessary and to the "Stencil Color Guide" provided on page 70. For detailed stenciling instructions, see "Stenciling" on pages 13–15.

7. To achieve the plaid effect on the back legs and stretchers, start by pouring a nickel-sized pool of Green Mist onto your palette. Add a couple of drops of extender and a few drops of water next to the paint. Drag your brush bristles across the three as you pick up paint in the next step. Diluting the paint in this manner will help you achieve smooth, continuous brush strokes.

8. Using a wing, comb, or rake brush, apply the paint to the back legs and stretchers. Hold the brush perpendicular to the chair's surface—not at an angle—and pull it horizontally across each surface. When these lines have dried, you can rake more paint—vertically, this time—over them.

9. Repeat steps 7 and 8 to apply French Grey Blue to all Uniform Blue areas, Forest Green to the edges of the seat that are painted with Green Mist, and Uniform Blue to the back skirt rail.

10. Using a cotton swab, apply Uniform Blue La De Da Dots to the center back slat. (See "La De Da Dots" on page 18.) Use an embossing tool to apply Antique White La De Da Dots to stretchers painted with Antique Maroon. For correct color placement, refer to the photo.

11. Use a black paint pen to write the words "Home Tweet Home" on the chair seat.

12. Sign your chair and allow all the paint to dry for several days. Then protect your work by applying at least 3 coats of varnish. (See "Final Touches" on page 19.) If your chair will rest outdoors, be sure to use exterior varnish.

13. Glue the buttons to the wooden stars and to the birdhouse roof. Glue the stars to the upper front face of 1 back leg, and glue the green moss onto the birdhouse base.

14. Have a woodworker attach the wooden dowel to the birdhouse base and mount the birdhouse on one back chair leg.

BASE-COAT COLOR GUIDE

CHAIR PARTS	COLORS
Birdhouse walls, top back slat, top of seat, front skirt rail	White Wash/Antique White
2 side stretchers (1 lower, 1 upper), back legs	Forest Green
2 vertical back slats, front legs, birdhouse roof	Uniform Blue
2 vertical back slats, front legs, back skirt rail	French Grey Blue
Bottom back slat, outer edges of seat	Green Mist
Top edges of seat, birdhouse base, dowel, wooden stars, front and back stretchers, and 2 side stretchers (1 lower, 1 upper)	Antique Maroon

STENCIL COLOR GUIDE

CHAIR PARTS	STENCILS	COLORS
Top back slat, birdhouse	Let's Be a Star	Antique Maroon, Uniform Blue
Bottom back slat	Flowers from Fresh Cherries	Antique Maroon, Evergreen, Antique White
Center of seat	Fergie's Birdhouse Collection	Forest Green, Green Mist, Uniform Blue, French Grey Blue, Antique Maroon, Evergreen, Burnt Umber, Black
Front and side skirt rails	Lil Checks	Antique Maroon

AMERICANA WITH ATTITUDE

TOOLS AND SUPPLIES

Required tools and supplies (see pages 6–8)

Artist's fan

Acrylic paints

To reproduce the photographed chair, use the DecoArt Americana paints listed below, or substitute other acrylic paints for a different look.

Desert Sand (DA77)—2 bottles

Country Red (DA18)

Admiral Blue (DA213)

White Wash (DA02)

Yellow Ochre (DA08)

Burnt Orange (DA16)

Marigold (DA194)

Evergreen (DA82)

White (DA01)

Black (DA67)

Easy Blend Charcoal Grey (DEB28)

Tomato Red (DA169)

Hauser Light Green (DA131)

Driftwood (DA171)

Hauser Medium Green (DA132)

Golden Straw (DA168)

Stencils

If you'd like to reproduce this chair exactly as it's shown, use the Stencilled Garden stencils listed here; they're available at specialty stencil stores and through mail-order suppliers. (See "Suppliers" on page 95.) For a different look, just substitute other stencils.

Penny's Poultry Gone Wild (TSG142)

Wild Posies (TSG190)

Curvy Checks (TSG715L)

Every Little Star (TSG832)

Buzzy Bee Border (TSG825)

American Pie (TSG238)

Summertime (TSG176)

Garden Critters (TSG140)

Lil Checks (TSG707)

INSTRUCTIONS

1. Prepare your chair for painting. (See "Chair Preparation" on pages 11–12.)
2. Apply as many base coats of Desert Sand as necessary to achieve smooth, opaque coverage on the entire chair. (See "Base-Coat Painting" on page 12.)
3. Use your artist's brushes to apply color washes. Refer to the "Color-Wash Guide" below. (Also see "Color Washing" on pages 15–16.)
4. Stencil the designs. Refer to the photos as necessary and to the "Stencil Color Guide" provided on page 73. For detailed stenciling instructions, see "Stenciling" on pages 13–15.
5. Pour a small amount of Country Red onto your palette and add an equal amount of water. Using your artist's fan, mix the paint and water together. With the handle of another brush, lightly tap the artist's fan handle to spatter most of the paint onto a paper towel. Then, holding the artist's fan over the chair seat, tap its handle lightly again to spatter paint onto the seat (see top of page 73).

COLOR-WASH GUIDE

CHAIR PARTS	COLORS
Top back slat, front legs, upper and lower back stretchers	Country Red
Back legs, upper and lower front stretchers	Admiral Blue
Seat, armrest, side stretchers	White Wash

While traveling through Texas on the way to a painting convention, we discovered many wonderful antique shops. Every time we saw the words "antiques and collectibles," we couldn't help ourselves; we had to stop. (Making a U-turn on a highway, with a trailer in tow, is challenging but not impossible!) This chair was one of several that we couldn't pass up; we had to get a bigger trailer for the return trip.

Spatter technique

6. Sign your chair and allow the paint to dry for several days. Then protect your work by applying at least 3 coats of varnish. (See "Final Touches" on page 19.)

STENCIL COLOR GUIDE

CHAIR PARTS	STENCILS	COLORS
Seat	Chicken from Penny's Poultry Gone Wild	Yellow Ochre, Admiral Blue, Country Red, Burnt Orange
	Flowers from Wild Posies, placed randomly	Marigold, Evergreen, Admiral Blue
Top back slat	Curvy Checks Stars from Every Little Star, placed randomly	Admiral Blue, Country Red, White
Bottom back slat	Bees from Buzzy Bee Border, placed randomly	Country Red, Black, White, Easy Blend Charcoal Grey
Armrest	Watermelon, flag, and chicken from American Pie	Tomato Red, Country Red, Admiral Blue, Black, Burnt Orange, White, Hauser Light Green, Driftwood, Hauser Medium Green, Golden Straw, Marigold, Evergreen, Easy Blend Charcoal Grey
	Stars from Every Little Star, placed randomly	Admiral Blue, Country Red, White
Back legs, outside edges	Watermelons from Summertime	Country Red, Hauser Light Green, Hauser Medium Green, Black
	Ants from Garden Critters	Black, Tomato Red
Skirt rails	Lil Checks	Admiral Blue
	Ladybugs from Summertime	Country Red, Hauser Light Green, Hauser Medium Green, Black
	Flowers from Wild Posies, placed randomly	Golden Straw, Marigold, Evergreen, Admiral Blue
Front legs	Stars from Every Little Star	Admiral Blue, Country Red, White

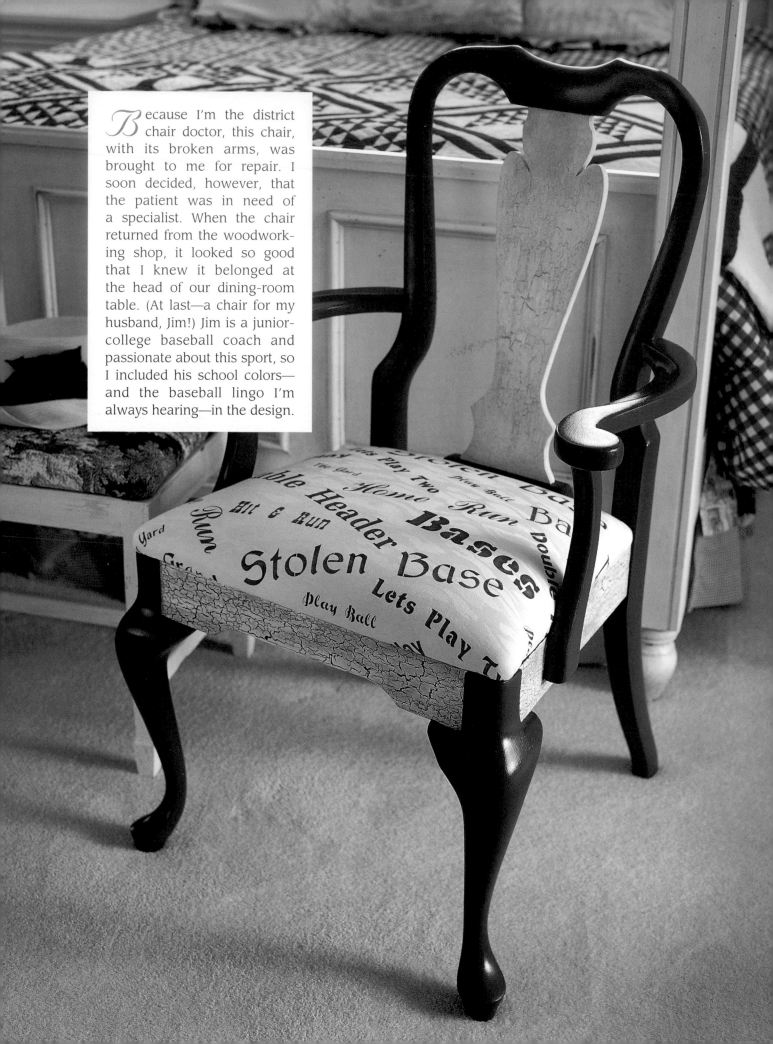

*B*ecause I'm the district chair doctor, this chair, with its broken arms, was brought to me for repair. I soon decided, however, that the patient was in need of a specialist. When the chair returned from the woodworking shop, it looked so good that I knew it belonged at the head of our dining-room table. (At last—a chair for my husband, Jim!) Jim is a junior-college baseball coach and passionate about this sport, so I included his school colors—and the baseball lingo I'm always hearing—in the design.

AGED IN TIME

TOOLS AND SUPPLIES

Required tools and supplies (see pages 6–8)
Screwdriver
Crackle medium
Fabric for seat
Fabric painting medium
Repositionable spray adhesive
Sheet of smooth cardboard
Press cloth
Iron
Gel stain (DS30)
Acrylic paints

To reproduce the photographed chair, use the DecoArt Americana paints listed below, or substitute other acrylic paints for a different look.

Country Red (DA18); 3 bottles
White (DA01)

Stencil

If you'd like to reproduce this chair exactly as it's shown, use the Stencilled Garden stencil listed here; it's available at specialty stencil stores and through mail-order suppliers. (See "Suppliers" on page 95.) For a different look, just substitute a different stencil.

The Olde Ball Game (TSG822)

INSTRUCTIONS

1. Remove the seat from your chair and set it aside.
2. Prepare your chair for painting. (See "Chair Preparation" on pages 11–12.)
3. Apply as many base coats of Country Red as necessary to achieve smooth, opaque coverage on all parts except the vertical back slat. Paint the back slat with White.
4. Using removable painter's tape, mask off all areas adjacent to the back slat and the 3 skirt rails.

5. Working on one small area at a time, apply crackle medium to the back slat and front and side skirt rails. Allow it to dry completely. (See "Crackle Finishes" on page 17.) Then apply a White topcoat over the crackle medium.

Side and back view

Back slat

Skirt rail

6. Prepare your fabric for painting. (See "Stenciling on Fabric" on page 15.)

7. On your palette, mix 2 parts Country Red paint with 1 part fabric painting medium. Placing the stenciled words randomly, stencil the new fabric with this mixture. When the paint has dried on the fabric, use a press cloth and iron to heat-set the paint.

8. To create an antique effect on the crackled areas, first apply varnish to them and let it dry. (See "Antique Finishes" on page 16.) Then, working one area at a time, apply gel stain and wipe it off.

9. Sign your chair and allow all the paint to dry for several days. Then protect your work by applying at least 3 coats of varnish. (See "Final Touches" on page 19.)

10. Take the chair, your new fabric, and the old seat to an upholsterer, who can make a new seat, cover it with your stenciled fabric, and attach the seat to the chair. (See "Final Touches" on page 19.)

Close-up of seat fabric

ALL CHECKED OUT

TOOLS AND SUPPLIES

Required tools and supplies (see pages 6–8)
Screwdriver
Transparent graph ruler
Watercolor pencil—yellow
1"-wide foam brush
Embossing tool
Fabric for seat
Acrylic paints

To reproduce the photographed chair, use the DecoArt Americana paints listed below, or substitute other acrylic paints for a different look.

Light Buttermilk (DA164)
White (DA01)
Shale Green (DA152)
Country Blue (DA41)
Moon Yellow (DA07)
Santa Red (DA170)
Evergreen (DA82)
Black (DA67)

Stencils

If you'd like to reproduce this chair exactly as it's shown, use the Stencilled Garden stencils listed here; they're available at specialty stencil stores and through mail-order suppliers. (See "Suppliers" on page 95.) For a different look, just substitute other stencils.

Cherries Jubilee (TSG184)
Girly's Flowers (TSG175)
Checkerboards (TSG706)
Ashley's Tea Party (TSG183)
Squiggles & Dots (TSG178)

INSTRUCTIONS

1. Remove the upholstered seat and set it aside.
2. Prepare the chair for painting. (See "Chair Preparation" on pages 11–12.)
3. Apply as many base coats as necessary to achieve smooth, opaque coverage on the entire chair. (See "Base-Coat Painting" on page 12.) For correct color placement, refer to the photos and to the "Base-Coat Color Guide" provided below.
4. Using your transparent graph ruler and a yellow watercolor pencil, mark 1"-wide vertical stripes on the front skirt rail. If your freehand painting skills aren't the best, use removable painter's tape to mask adjacent areas before painting them. (See "Stripes" on pages 17–18.)
5. On your palette, dilute some Moon Yellow paint with water. Then use a 1"-wide foam brush to paint every other marked stripe. Allow the paint to dry well and remove the tape if you've used any.
6. Stencil the designs. Refer to the photos as necessary and to the "Stencil Color Guide" provided on page 79. For detailed stenciling instructions, see "Stenciling" on pages 13–15.

BASE-COAT COLOR GUIDE

CHAIR PARTS	COLORS
Top back slat, skirt rails	Light Buttermilk
Center back slat, stretchers	White
Back legs	Shale Green
Front legs	Country Blue

THE QUEEN HAS ARRIVED

To complete my collection of four family chairs for our dining room, I painted this one for myself. I used my favorite designs and colors, and I had so much fun working on the chair that I even painted and stenciled the underside of the seat. I still have fun painting, even after all the years I've spent doing it.

Top back slat

Stretchers and front leg

Skirt rail

7. Using an embossing tool, paint Black La De Da Dots on the top back slat, the front skirt rail, and the front legs. (See "La De Da Dots" on page 18.) Refer to the photos for placement.

8. Sign your chair and allow all the paint to dry for several days. Then protect your work by applying at least 3 coats of varnish. (See "Final Touches" on page 19.)

9. Take the chair, your new fabric, and the old seat to an upholsterer, who can make a new seat, cover it with your fabric, and attach the seat to the chair. (See "Final Touches" on page 19.)

STENCIL COLOR GUIDE

CHAIR PARTS	STENCILS	COLORS
Top back slat, skirt rails	Cherries Jubilee Girly's Flowers	Santa Red, Evergreen Evergreen, Country Blue
Center back slat	Checkerboards: 1"	Black
Stretchers	Checkerboards: ¾"	Santa Red
Front legs	Flowers from Ashley's Tea Party	Moon Yellow, Evergreen, Santa Red
Back legs	Squiggles from Squiggles & Dots	Black

While Judy was heading toward the coast to visit her daughter, Corri (at that time, the mother-to-be of Samantha), and Corri's husband, Bob, she couldn't resist stopping at one of her favorite junk stores. It's a good thing she did! She'd have hated to miss this chair.

JUBEE'S THRONE

TOOLS AND SUPPLIES

Required tools and supplies (see pages 6–8)
Screwdriver
Embossing tool
Cotton swabs
Fabric for seat
Acrylic paints

To reproduce the photographed chair, use the DecoArt Americana paints listed below, or substitute other acrylic paints for a different look.

Santa Red (DA170)
White (DA01)
Country Blue (DA41)
Black (DA67)
French Vanilla (DA184)
Light Buttermilk (DA164)
Raspberry (DA28)
Olive Green (DA56)
Evergreen (DA82)
Marigold (DA194)
Hauser Medium Green (DA132)

Stencils

If you'd like to reproduce this chair exactly as it's shown, use the Stencilled Garden stencils listed here; they're available at specialty stencil stores and through mail-order suppliers. (See "Suppliers" on page 95.) For a different look, just substitute other stencils.

Squiggles & Dots (TSG178)
Checkerboards (TSG706)
Cherries Jubilee (TSG184)
Ashley's Tea Party (TSG183)
Lil Checks (TSG707)
Summertime (TSG176)
Gone '60s (TSG816)
Garden Critters (TSG140)
Girly's Flowers (TSG175)

INSTRUCTIONS

1. Remove the seat from your chair and set it aside.
2. Prepare your chair for painting. (See "Chair Preparation" on pages 11–12.)

BASE-COAT COLOR GUIDE

CHAIR PARTS	COLORS
Top back slat, back legs, center stretcher	Santa Red
Center back slat	White
Bottom back slat	Country Blue
Side stretchers (one end to the other)	Country Blue, Black, Country Blue
Armrests	French Vanilla
Side and back skirt rails	Light Buttermilk
Front skirt rail (top to bottom)	Light Buttermilk, Raspberry, Light Buttermilk
Vertical arm spindles (top to bottom)	Country Blue, Black, Olive Green, Raspberry
Front legs (top to bottom)	Black, Country Blue, Santa Red, Olive Green, Raspberry, Black

3. Apply as many base coats as necessary to achieve smooth, opaque coverage on the entire chair. (See "Base-Coat Painting" on page 12.) For correct color placement, refer to the photos and to the "Base-Coat Color Guide" provided on page 81.

4. Stencil the designs. Refer to the photos as necessary and to the "Stencil Color Guide" provided below. For detailed instructions, see "Stenciling" on pages 13–15. Here's one important tip: When you're stenciling over a dark color such as the black checks on this chair, stencil the design with White paint first and then apply your colors on top of the White. If you skip this step, your colors won't show up on the dark background.

Back skirt rail

Side skirt rail

5. Using an embossing tool, paint French Vanilla La De Da Dots around the cherries. (See La De Da Dots on page 18). With the same tool, paint White La De Da Dots on the tops and bottoms of the front legs. Using a cotton swab, paint Black La De Da Dots on the back skirt rail, armrests, and center stretcher.

6. Sign your chair and allow all the paint to dry for several days. Then protect your work by applying at least 3 coats of varnish. (See "Final Touches" on page 19.)

7. Take the chair, your new fabric, and the old seat to an upholsterer, who can make a new seat, cover it with your fabric, and attach the seat to the chair. (See "Final Touches" on page 19.)

STENCIL COLOR GUIDE

CHAIR PARTS	STENCILS	COLORS
Top back slat, back legs	Squiggles from Squiggles & Dots	Black
Center back slat	Checkerboards: 1½"	Black
	Cherries Jubilee	Santa Red, Evergreen
Bottom back slat, top corners of front legs, centers of side stretchers	Flowers from Ashley's Tea Party	Evergreen, French Vanilla, Raspberry
Front skirt rail	Lil Checks	Black
Side skirt rails	Watermelons from Summertime, placed randomly Ladybugs from Garden Critters, placed randomly	Santa Red, Marigold, Hauser Medium Green, Black
Back skirt rail	Gone '60s	Country Blue, Olive Green, Black
Armrests	Girly's Flowers	Country Blue, Evergreen

SPINDLED ROYALTY

TOOLS AND SUPPLIES

Required tools and supplies (see pages 6–8)
Screwdriver
Transparent graph ruler
Watercolor pencil—yellow
1"-wide foam brush
Fabric for seat
Fabric painting medium
Repositionable spray adhesive
Sheet of smooth cardboard
Transparent fabric medium
Press cloth
Iron
Embossing tool
Cotton swabs
Acrylic paints

> To reproduce the photographed chair, use the DecoArt Americana paints listed below, or substitute other acrylic paints for a different look.

Country Blue (CA41)
French Vanilla (DA184)
French Mauve (DA186)
Cranberry Wine (DA112)
White (DA01)
Hauser Light Green (DA131)
Mauve (DA26)
Evergreen (DA82)
Violet Haze (DA197)
Black (DA67)
Yellow Ochre (DA08)
Stencils

> If you'd like to reproduce this chair exactly as it's shown, use the Stencilled Garden stencils listed here; they're available at specialty stencil stores and through mail-order suppliers. (See "Suppliers" on page 95.) For a different look, just substitute other stencils.

Squiggles & Dots (TSG178)
Girly's Flower Border (TSG122)
Ashley's Tea Party (TSG183)
Girly's Flowers (TSG175)
Girly's Gone Checked (TSG222)
Two for Tea (TSG237)

INSTRUCTIONS

1. Remove the seat from your chair and set it aside.
2. Prepare your chair for painting. (See "Chair Preparation" on pages 11–12.)
3. Apply as many base coats as necessary to achieve smooth, opaque coverage on the

BASE-COAT COLOR GUIDE

CHAIR PARTS	COLORS
Top back slat	Country Blue
Center back slat, side stretchers	French Vanilla
Back legs	French Mauve
Horizontal arms	Cranberry Wine
Skirt rails	White
Arm spindles (top to bottom)	French Vanilla, Country Blue, French Mauve, Hauser Light Green
Front legs (top to bottom)	Cranberry Wine, French Vanilla, Country Blue, Mauve, Cranberry Wine, Hauser Light Green, French Mauve

Judy not only found this unusual chair, she also found its matched partner. The chairs' great designs made their price a little too high, but Judy asked for the friendliest price and managed to get a great deal. We painted one of the matched set as a gift for Judy's daughter, Corri, and the other for Judy herself. The chairs' wonderful spindled legs demanded multiple colors, of course.

entire chair. (See "Base-Coat Painting" on page 12.) For correct color placement, refer to the photos and to the "Base-Coat Color Guide" provided on page 83.

4. Using your transparent graph ruler and watercolor pencil, mark 1"-wide vertical stripes on all 4 skirt rails. You may want to use removable painter's tape to mask off the edges of the stripes before painting them. (See "Stripes" on pages 17–18.)

5. On your palette, dilute some French Vanilla with water. Then use a 1"-wide foam brush to paint the stripes. When the paint has dried, remove the tape.

6. Stencil the designs. Refer to the photos as necessary and to the "Stencil Color Guide" provided below. For detailed stenciling instructions, see "Stenciling" on pages 13–15.

7. Prepare your fabric for painting. (See "Stenciling on Fabric" on page 15.)

8. Working with one color at a time, on your palette, mix 2 parts paint with 1 part fabric painting medium. Stencil the Girly's Gone Checked pattern first with French Mauve, Mauve, and Evergreen. Then use Hauser Light Green, French Mauve, Violet Haze, French Vanilla, Cranberry Wine, and Evergreen with the Two for Tea stencil.

9. On your palette, mix 6 parts transparent fabric medium with 1 part Hauser Light Green. Using a stencil brush, scrub this wash into the fabric around all the stenciling.

10. Allow all the paint to dry on the fabric. Then heat-set the paint by covering it with a press cloth and heating the cloth with an iron.

11. Using an embossing tool and cotton swabs, paint La De Da Dots in White, Black, Yellow Ochre, Cranberry Wine, and Mauve. (See La De Da Dots on page 18.) Refer to the photos for correct placement.

12. Sign your chair and allow all the paint to dry for several days. Then protect your work by applying at least 3 coats of varnish. (See "Final Touches" on page 19.)

13. Take the chair, your stenciled fabric, and the old seat to an upholsterer, who can make a new seat, cover it with your stenciled fabric, and attach the seat to the chair. (See "Final Touches" on page 19.)

Skirt rail

STENCIL COLOR GUIDE

CHAIR PARTS	STENCILS	COLORS
Top back slat, side stretchers, flat-sided sections of front legs	Squiggles from Squiggles & Dots	French Vanilla, Cranberry Wine
Center back slat	Flowers from Girly's Flower Border, placed randomly	Country Blue, Evergreen, Hauser Light Green
Back legs	Flowers from Ashley's Tea Party, placed randomly	French Vanilla, Country Blue, Cranberry Wine, Evergreen
Skirt rails	Girly's Flowers	Country Blue, Evergreen

We originally bought an old chair much like the one shown here, but it needed a lot of work because it was so rusty. By chance, we then found a brand-new chair just like it, but minus the rust; it just needed to be assembled. Needless to say, we may never paint the old, rusty chair.

A DAY IN THE GARDEN

TOOLS AND SUPPLIES

Required tools and supplies (see pages 6–8)
Acrylic paints

To reproduce the photographed chair, use the DecoArt Americana paints listed below, or substitute other acrylic paints for a different look.

Limeade (DA206)—3 bottles
Buttermilk (DA03)
Sand (DA04)
Desert Sand (DA77)
Pansy Lavender (DA154)
Royal Purple (DA150)
Easy Blend Charcoal Grey (DEB28)
Summer Lilac (DA189)
Light Avocado (DA106)
Avocado (DA52)
Grey Sky (DA111)
Slate Grey (DA68)
Black (DA67)
White (DA01)
Moon Yellow (DA07)
Marigold (DA194)

Stencils

If you'd like to reproduce this chair exactly as it's shown, use the Stencilled Garden stencils listed here; they're available at specialty stencil stores and through mail-order suppliers. (See "Suppliers" on page 95.) For a different look, just substitute other stencils.

Mother's Hats and Pearls (TSG905)
Garden Gloves (TSG213)
Garden Tools (TSG214)
Hungry Kitty (TSG720)

INSTRUCTIONS

1. Prepare your chair for painting. (See "Chair Preparation" on pages 11–12.)
2. Apply as many Limeade base coats as necessary to achieve smooth, opaque coverage on the entire chair. (See "Base-Coat Painting" on page 12.) Allow the paint to dry.
3. Stencil the designs. Refer to the photos as necessary and to the "Stencil Color Guide"

STENCIL COLOR GUIDE

CHAIR PARTS	STENCILS	COLORS
Back	Mother's Hats and Pearls	Buttermilk, Sand, Desert Sand, Pansy Lavender, Royal Purple, Easy Blend Charcoal Grey
Seat	Garden Gloves	Summer Lilac, Pansy Lavender, Royal Purple, Easy Blend Charcoal Grey
	Garden Tools	Light Avocado, Avocado, Grey Sky, Slate Grey
	Hungry Kitty	Black, White, Moon Yellow, Marigold, Easy Blend Charcoal Grey

provided on page 87. For detailed stenciling instructions, see "Stenciling" on pages 13–15. Here's a tip: To overlap 2 designs, first stencil the one that will appear to be "underneath," such as the Garden Gloves design on this chair seat. When the paint is dry, position the second stencil (in this case, the Garden Tools) so that it overlaps the first design. Using White paint, stencil over all portions of the first design that show through the second stencil's design windows. When the White paint has dried, stencil the second design.

4. Sign your chair and allow all the paint to dry for several days. Then protect your work by applying at least 3 coats of varnish. (See "Final Touches" on page 19.)

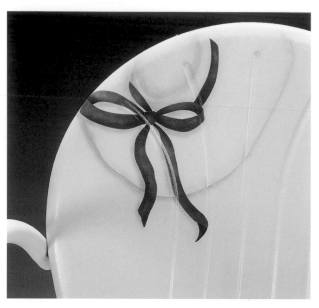

Stenciled hat on chair back

Seat

TAKE A NOTE

TOOLS AND SUPPLIES

Required tools and supplies (see pages 6–8)
Screwdriver
Gel stain (DS30)
Fabric for seat
Acrylic paints

To reproduce the photographed chair, use the DecoArt Americana paints listed below, or substitute other acrylic paints for a different look.

Black Plum (DA172)
Antique White (DA58)—2 bottles
White (DA01)
Jade Green (DA57)
Evergreen (DA82)
Plum (DA175)
Easy Blend Charcoal Grey (DEB28)

Stencils

If you'd like to reproduce this chair exactly as it's shown, use the Stencilled Garden stencils listed here; they're available at specialty stencil stores and through mail-order suppliers. (See "Suppliers" on page 95.) For a different look, just substitute other stencils.

Ashley Morgan's Lace (TSG158)
Rose and Card (TSG604)

INSTRUCTIONS

1. Remove the seat from your chair and set it aside.
2. Prepare your chair for painting. (See "Chair Preparation" on pages 11–12.)
3. Apply as many base coats as necessary to achieve smooth, opaque coverage on the entire chair. (See "Base-Coat Painting" on page 12.) For correct color placement, refer to the photos and to the "Base-Coat Color Guide" provided below.

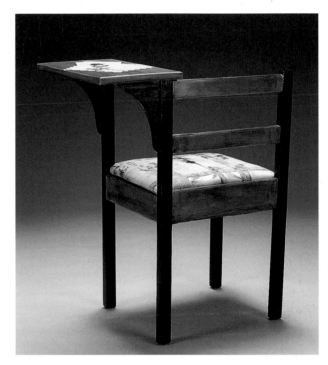

Back view

4. Apply a Black Plum color wash over all the sections of the chair that you painted with an Antique White base coat. (See "Color Washing" on pages 15–16.)
5. On the desktop, stencil Ashley Morgan's Lace with White paint. Move the stencil around to create the doily design.

BASE-COAT COLOR GUIDE

CHAIR PARTS	COLORS
Legs and desk brackets	Black Plum
All other areas	Antique White

We found this chair during a one-day "junking trip" break from a painting convention. Because we were flying home, we couldn't buy many chairs, but when we discovered this one—and the fact that it was a "lefty"—we just couldn't leave it behind. We somehow managed to find and dismantle enough boxes to wrap the chair, and we shipped it back home. Although we usually select a fabric to complement a chair's painted design, the fabric for this chair inspired the designs.

6. To create an antique look on the stenciled doily, brush on and wipe off some gel stain. Omit the coat of varnish that is usually applied under a gel stain. (See "Antique Finishes" on page 16.)

7. Shield the stenciled doily design by placing the solid, positive (or "fallout") portion of the Ashley Morgan's Lace stencil over it. (This stencil comes with both positive and negative pieces.) Then position the note card and envelope portions of the Rose and Card stencil on top of the fallout. Stencil the note card with White and the envelope with Buttermilk onto the unshielded area of the desktop. Using a fallout in this fashion will make the stenciled note card and envelope appear to be underneath the doily.

8. Using Jade Green, Evergreen, Plum, and Black Plum, stencil the rose from the Rose and Card stencil. Place the rose on top of the doily.

9. To create the shadow effect around the doily, leave the fallout in place and stencil around its outer edges with Easy Blend Charcoal Grey and Black Plum. Alternatively, remove the stencil and use a ¼"-wide artist's brush for freehand application of the Easy Blend Charcoal Grey.

10. Sign your chair and allow all the paint to dry for several days. Then protect your work by applying at least 3 coats of varnish. (See "Final Touches" on page 19.)

11. Take the chair, your new fabric, and the old seat to an upholsterer, who can make a new seat, cover it with your fabric, and attach the seat to the chair. (See "Final Touches" on page 19.)

Stenciled armrest

This project is one of a pair of old bar stools that were in need of a fresh, new look. We now take them both to all the painting conventions and trade shows we attend. Remember: When a chair's painted design becomes dated or no longer pleases you, don't get rid of the chair. Just take out all your supplies and create a new look.

PLANT YOUR SEAT

TOOLS AND SUPPLIES

Required tools and supplies (see pages 6–8)
Acrylic paints

To reproduce the photographed chair, use the DecoArt Americana paints listed below, or substitute other acrylic paints for a different look.

White (DA01)
Santa Red (DA170)
Black (DA67)
Moon Yellow (CA07)
Jade Green (DA57)
Evergreen (DA82)
Napa Red (DA165)
Black Plum (DA172)
Country Blue (DA41)
Hauser Light Green (DA131)
Easy Blend Charcoal Grey (DEB 28)

Stencils

If you'd like to reproduce this chair exactly as it's shown, use the Stencilled Garden stencils listed here; they're available at specialty stencil stores and through mail-order suppliers. (See "Suppliers" on page 95.) For a different look, just substitute other stencils.

Lil Checks (TSG707)
J.F. Seed Co. (TSG236)

INSTRUCTIONS

1. Prepare your chair for painting. (See "Chair Preparation" on pages 11–12.)

2. Apply as many base coats as necessary to achieve smooth, opaque coverage on the entire chair. (See "Base-Coat Painting" on page 12.) For correct color placement, refer to the photos and to the "Base-Coat Color Guide" provided below.

3. Stencil the designs. Refer to the photos as necessary and to the "Stencil Color Guide" provided on page 94. For detailed instructions, see "Stenciling" on pages 13–15. Here are a couple of tips before you begin: To overlap the 2 seed-packet designs on the seat, first stencil the packet that will appear to be on top. When the paint has dried, shield the stenciled design by placing the solid, positive (or "fallout") portion of the stencil over it. Position the next seed-packet stencil on top, and stencil the second seed packet. Using the fallout will make this packet appear to be under the first packet. To create the shadows around the packets, leave the fallouts in place and stencil around their edges with Easy Blend Charcoal Grey.

Edge of seat

BASE-COAT COLOR GUIDE	
CHAIR PARTS	**COLORS**
Seat and 4 stretchers	White
4 stretchers	Santa Red
Legs	Black

Top of seat

4. Sign your chair and allow all the paint to dry for several days. Then protect your work by applying at least 3 coats of varnish. (See "Final Touches" on page 19.)

STENCIL COLOR GUIDE

CHAIR PARTS	STENCILS	COLORS
Edge of seat	Lil Checks	Santa Red
Top of seat	Seed packets from J.F. Seed Co.	Santa Red, White, Black, Moon Yellow, Jade Green, Evergreen, Napa Red, Black Plum, Country Blue, Hauser Light Green, Easy Blend Charcoal Grey

SUPPLIERS

The Stencilled Garden
6029 N. Palm Avenue
Fresno, CA 93704
(559) 449-7711
Web site: www.stencilledgarden.com

*Stencils, paints, brushes, and other
decorative painting supplies*

DecoArt
P.O. Box 386
Stanford, KY 40484
(800) 367-3047
Web site: www.decoart.com

*Acrylic paints, gel stains, varnish, glazes, and
other decorative painting supplies*

Eagle Brush Company
431 Commerce Park Drive S.E.
Suites 100 & 101
Marietta, GA 30060
(800) 832-4532

Artist's brushes

ABOUT THE AUTHORS

Judy Skinner and Jennifer Ferguson

An artist, designer, and teacher of the arts of stenciling and faux finishing, Jennifer Ferguson has been painting projects for the past twelve years. Through her company, The Stencilled Garden, she designs stencils, teaches stenciling and faux finishing, and sells stenciling and faux-finishing supplies. Jennifer has appeared on *The Carol Duvall Show*, *Aleene's Creative Living*, and the *Kitty Bartholomew Show*, where she shared some of her ideas and projects with viewers. When she isn't attending trade shows or painting projects, Jennifer enjoys spending time with her family and working on their new home.

An artist, "house stripper," and recycler, Judy Skinner has been creating art for more than twenty years. Through her own company, Collectiques by Jubee, she recycles old windows, doors, drawers, and any other house parts she can find by transforming them into works of art that she sells at art shows throughout California and Nevada. When she isn't attending art shows or finding houses to strip, Judy enjoys spending time with her family and finishing projects for their home.

Jennifer and Judy met at Jennifer's shop back in 1996, and they've developed a wonderful friendship since then. Their mutual love for the arts of recycling, painting, stenciling, and faux finishing gives them much to share. They travel all over the United States to attend conventions, and they have taken these great opportunities to indulge in "junking" trips and to find many treasures. *Painted Chairs* is the first of many projects they're working on. They both hope that you enjoy this book—and that you learn to love painting chairs as much as they do.